MADE E-Z
PRODUCTS

Organizing Your Home Business

Lisa Kanarek

Made E-Z

MADE E-Z PRODUCTS™ Inc.
Deerfield Beach, Florida / www.MadeE-Z.com

Published by:

 384 South Military Trail
Deerfield Beach, FL 33442

http://www.MadeE-Z.com

1 2 3 4 5 6 7 8 9 10

Organizing Your Home Business Made E-Z™
Lisa Kanarek

ABOUT LISA KANAREK

Lisa Kanarek is one of the nation's leading home office experts and the author of *Home Office Life: Making a Space to Work at Home, 101 Home Office Success Secrets* and *Everything's Organized.* She is the founder of HomeOfficeLife.com, a firm that advises corporations and individuals on all aspects of working from home including physical set-up, technology, productivity and transitioning from a corporate office to a home office.

Kanarek is a frequent speaker to Fortune 500 corporations and a regular contributor to national and international publications. Her clients include American Airlines, Avery, Fellowes, Fuji, Hallmark Cards, Johnson & Johnson, JC Penney, Lexmark, Microsoft, Office Depot, Sprint, Texas Instruments and Volkswagen, among others.

Kanarek has been a guest on several national programs including *Good Morning America*, CBS *Up-to-the-Minute*,  CNBC, American Public Radio, Public Radio's *Marketplace* and *Voice of America* radio. Articles by and about Kanarek have appeared in hundreds of publications including *The Wall Street Journal, Home Office Computing, The New York Times, Newsweek, Success, Money, Entrepreneur, Cosmopolitan, Home Office Computing, Working at Home, Working Woman, Marie Claire, Redbook* and *Nation's Business*.

Table of Contents

To my family who inspires me daily—
my husband, Gary Weinstein, and our sons, Blake and Kyle.

Introduction

Corporate America is moving home. The work that used to be done in high-rise office buildings is now being done in kitchens, basements, spare rooms, even corners of rooms, all over the country. Computers, fax machines, and the Internet make it possible to do almost any work in a home office that can be done in a corporate office. This is changing the ways in which both corporations and individuals get things done.

Who's working at home

There are over 34 million home office households in the United States today. Everyone from displaced corporate executives to the President of the United States has a home office.

There are a number of reasons why corporations are more and more willing to set up employees in home offices. Home-based corporate employees save companies from having to pay high overhead costs. National companies are finding that maintaining representatives all over the country not only allows them to reach a wider talent base, it enables them to serve local clients better, and these representatives can still stay in close touch with management by means of electronic mail and cost-effective teleconferencing. Companies of all sizes are finding that allowing workers to split their time between a corporate office and a home office keeps talented employees (and often new mothers) happy, with a minimum of disruptions, which saves the expense of finding and training new people.

Added to the ranks of corporate employees who work at home are the ever-growing numbers of self-employed people, including consultants, financial planners, physicians, lawyers, writers, artists, and freelancers of all types. Some home office professionals have worked in corporate offices—some haven't. Some moonlight out of home offices but have different jobs during the day. Others have set up cottage industries at home or have started an informal, small business that is rapidly becoming bigger and more time-consuming. Today retirees are starting new, home-based careers—mothers are interested in working at home so that they can be near their children and corporate employees who were laid off during company downsizing are deciding to set up shop for themselves instead of going back to the nine-to-five lifestyle. All of these people have found that maintaining an office at home beats paying high rents for space elsewhere and offers other advantages, which you'll learn more about later.

Home office organizing

There is a catch. Running a home office is not like running a corporate office, or, for that matter, like running a home. My specialty is creating productive home offices and home-based businesses, and over the years I've noticed that home offices present certain unique challenges. The home office professionals who recognize and deal with these challenges are more effective and more in control—and therefore less stressed, less frustrated, and more successful at what they do, than those who don't.

I'd like to share with you the guidelines and recommendations I give my clients and audiences during seminars so that you can spend less time fighting meaningless battles with your papers and more time on productive work. This book will give you the direction you need to do the following:

- Set up an efficient home office
- Eliminate office clutter
- Reduce the time you spend looking for important information
- Streamline incoming information, both paper-based and electronic
- Set up a tailor-made filing system
- Make the most of home office technology
- Take control of your time and increase your productivity
- Balance your business and personal life
- Increase your professionalism
- Focus on your priorities and goals
- Respond swiftly to new developments

In order to be truly productive, you need to be one step ahead of events, instead of always just reacting to what each day brings. By implementing the suggestions in this book, you'll find that you finally have the time you need to get caught up, to think creatively, to meet more challenges, and to do whatever it is you want to do.

The secret to making your home office work for you is to organize it and keep it organized. I've written this book to get you on the right track and to keep you moving forward. It's like having your own home office expert with you 24 hours a day.

I can't organize you—only you can. What I can do is provide you with the tools and the information you need to get organized and maintain a comfortable level of organization. Although I have a lot to say about how to do things, I'd like you to remember that the point really isn't the process, but the results you'll get.

Taking control

In a corporate setting, you get a day's pay whether or not you accomplish a day's worth of work. When you work at home, any time you waste eventually will be reflected in your income, whether you spend half an hour talking on the phone with a friend or 15 minutes looking for a misplaced brochure. Your income is directly related to how productive you are.

As a home office professional, you can't rely upon other people to help you with your productivity. You're on your own. The bottom line is that in order to take control of your work, you first have to take control of your office.

Even if you're already organized—and most of the home office professionals I've met are smart, capable people—I guarantee you'll learn new methods you can use to fine-tune your approach.

Usually making adjustments to your working style is more effective than trying to make drastic changes. Keeping up with the latest office products is part of my job, so you'll also learn about some helpful items you may never have known existed.

For those of you who are ashamed of your home office because it's such a mess, take heart: you've come to the right book. No matter how bad you think your office is, I've seen worse.

One client actually hired me because she was afraid of what others would think of her if she died suddenly and they discovered what a mess her desk was! She was ashamed of how disorganized she was and, on a deeper level, felt ineffectual and out of control. Fortunately we were able to get her on track and she lived to enjoy the benefits of an organized home office.

This book is not about how to start or run a home-based business. My second book, *101 Home Office Success Secrets*, covers that. Instead, I'll show you organizing methods that every home office professional can apply to his or her work in order to become more efficient, more productive, and more successful.

Different people, different styles

Corporate offices are always somewhat alike, but home offices vary. Your home office reflects your style and personality, and while it makes sense to you, it might drive someone else crazy. Similarly, an organizational method that works for you could be totally inappropriate for someone else. For this reason, I always give you options from which to choose. If you're the type of person who uses a free-association approach to filing (like my client who had a "When I Feel Like It" file), don't bother trying to implement the numerical filing system presented in Chapter 9. Instead, a categorical system combined with colors could be perfect for you.

I don't like to take a rigid approach to anything, and I don't always agree with what other experts have to say. For example, it's often said that you should handle each piece of paper just once. If you act on it right away, the theory goes, you'll get more done, and papers won't be around long enough to clutter up your life. But how reasonable is this? In my view, not very reasonable. It sounds good, but it doesn't work. I'm only going to suggest proven methods that have worked for my clients and that can work for you, too.

Being exceptionally neat actually has nothing to do with being efficient. Although I enjoy being organized, I'm not going to tell you that you have to empty out your junk drawer or line up your pencils from shortest to longest. Being a perfectionist is counterproductive because obsessing over details takes time away from working. Although I do want you to get organized, my goal is to show you how to stay focused on your work and spend a minimum of time on nonsense.

How to use this book

Authors always hope readers will read their book from beginning to end, and I'm no exception. However, if you must dip into just the sections you think you need, I hope you'll at least skim the rest of the book, because you never know where you'll find a tip that will work for you. After you have read and used this book, it should be dog-eared, marked, and highlighted. That's the only way you're going to get completely organized.

I hope that once you get started, you'll continue to reinforce what you should be doing by referring to the book later. I've used lists and numbered steps wherever possible so that you can read and review the book quickly.

Each chapter of *Organizing Your Home Business Made E-Z* is dedicated to a particular aspect of organizing that is important to home office professionals. In addition, I've included a resource guide and product guide at the back of the book that will direct you to sources of further information.

If you want to get organized or be better organized, you can do it. Clients of mine whose offices weren't under control have been amazed at their new level of productivity after becoming organized. Many have said they wondered how they ever functioned before. Getting organized is a lot like changing to a healthy diet or getting onto a household budget—once you've made it a habit, it becomes easy to maintain.

So let's get started, and before you know it, you won't recognize your own office. In fact, I recommend that you take a picture of your office (or soon-to-be office) now and another when you've finished. The difference between the way it looks now and the way it will look after you've finished organizing it will astonish you.

The Challenges and Rewards of Working at Home

1

The Challenges and Rewards of Working at Home

Working at home has both advantages and challenges. Many aspects of working at home work both ways, with both a pleasant side and a downside. By implementing some special organizing methods that work for home office professionals, you can maximize the advantages and meet the challenges of a home office successfully.

This chapter will alert you to some of the special considerations that are part of working at home. Throughout the rest of the book, we'll find out how to effectively handle each one.

Switching from a corporate office to a home office

Advantage: *You're independent.*

Challenge: *You probably don't have any of the on-site support services you had in a corporate office.*

Working at home is not at all like working in a corporate office. If you're switching from a corporate setting to a home office, first spend some time analyzing the biggest conveniences of your corporate arrangement. What are you really going to miss about it? In what ways does the corporate setting work for you? How are you going to compensate for those advantages at home?

The Challenges and Rewards of Working at Home

When Janie, a medical representative, started working out of her home, it seemed as if her personality had changed along with her office location. In her corporate office, Janie had been extremely efficient and organized. Her desk had always been clear, and whenever anyone needed anything, they knew Janie would be able to find it in her files immediately. After just 30 days at home, Janie's desk in her bedroom was overflowing, and she had supplies and papers stashed all over the house. She was spending too much time running around trying to find things and trying to find places to put things.

Changing your environment changes the way you work. In Janie's case, switching to a home environment meant she no longer had a spacious office in which to store everything, she no longer had an administrative assistant to help her keep up with the typing, filing, paperwork, and phone calls, and she no longer had access to time-saving conveniences such as the "industrial strength" copier. Janie was having trouble maintaining both her standards and her pace.

When I first met with Janie, I knew right away she would have to find a better location for her home office so that she could consolidate her files and supplies. By putting a hideaway bed in the spare bedroom (see page 34), we freed up enough space for her to have a bona fide office. From there we worked on innovative storage techniques, using some old furniture in new ways, as well as adding more equipment including a copier.

After her office overhaul, Janie was ecstatic. She had always been an organized person, but working out of a makeshift home office had overwhelmed her.

I've seen many talented executives undermine new home-based careers by underestimating how much time it will take them to juggle the roles of errand runner, administrative assistant, receptionist, mail room clerk, and purchasing department head—not to mention sales and marketing manager.

> All home office professionals have to wear several hats, but those who are self-employed have the most demands of their time.

When Barry, a vice president of an electronics firm, retired from his corporate job, he decided to open a consulting firm in his home. Although he was well organized, had a well-equipped home office, had plenty of clients, and had the skills to be a consultant, there was a fatal flaw in Barry's business plan. He couldn't type. Barry had figured that typing couldn't be too difficult. Besides, didn't he have a spell checker on his computer? To his dismay, he discovered that a single letter was taking him an entire hour. We found Barry an administrative support service to help him handle his correspondence and proposals, which not only freed up a lot of Barry's time, it removed a source of irritation from his day.

If you've never worked in a corporate office

Advantage: *You can cultivate good home office work habits from the beginning.*

Challenge: *Starting from scratch can be overwhelming and usually involves making unnecessary mistakes.*

Those of you who have never worked in a corporate setting are lucky. You won't need to change any bad habits, and you won't miss the perks. However, you also don't have any model to follow as you set up your own office at home.

Carol, a client of mine, has a creative flair. When her children were growing up, she would hand paint T-shirts and give them away as birthday presents. Often her friends would say, "You know, you really ought to sell these." After hearing this for the fiftieth time, Carol decided her friends had a point, and she opened her own T-shirt business.

Success came too quickly. Carol was strong on T-shirts but not much on tracking accounts receivable or preparing tax records. All she wanted to do was decorate a few shirts and make a little money, but almost immediately the "business" side of her business started to drive her crazy. We spent an entire week setting up a home office for Carol and designing a filing system that would help her keep her accounts organized. Now her paperwork is taking up much less of her time, and she is finding her business fun again.

QUICK TIP FOR HOME OFFICE PROFESSIONALS

Take the time to get organized. In the long run, you'll come out ahead. Many people find it hard to take time off from working to see what they need to change about their methods. This is especially true of people who are already basically organized. However, just as it takes money to make money, it also takes time to save time. Motivating idea: every improvement you make will have an effect on the bottom line of your business.

Setting up your home office

Advantages: *Low overhead. Freedom to furnish your office however you wish.*

Challenges: *Carving an office out of living space in your home. Paying for all of your own equipment.*

One advantage of working at home is that you have low overhead because you aren't paying rent or a mortgage on office space elsewhere. On the other hand, you have to create an office somewhere within your home, which may mean making do with a cramped space or working around the needs (and mess!) of the rest of your family.

> Although you may need to be extremely resourceful, it is possible to set up an efficient office in an odd space or in a room that does double duty as something else.

As a home office professional, you can furnish your office however you like. This helps make your office an enjoyable place in which to spend time, and if you're in a creative profession, it may help you think in innovative ways. The downside of furnishing your workspace yourself is that you may have to buy all of your own office equipment, including supplies, furniture, and electronics. This quickly becomes very expensive. By making your choices carefully, you can get the most out of each expense.

For example, maybe a combination fax/copier/printer would be cost effective for you, or perhaps a lateral file cabinet that doubles as a functional work surface could save you the cost of an extra table.

I've found that most people who work at home basically let their office create itself. Piece by piece they add equipment—a fax machine, a computer work station, some shelves, and so on—until their office evolves into a workspace that suits their needs, but is less efficient than it could be. Using this book, I'd like you either to start off right with a comprehensive plan for your new home office, or, if you already have an office at home, to take a fresh look at how you might make the most of it.

Working unsupervised

Advantage: *No boss looking over your shoulder.*

Challenge: *Disciplining yourself.*

> It takes a particular personality to succeed in a home-based job.

If you're a good self-motivator, you may love being your own boss (or if you work for a corporation, not having a boss physically present) so much that you'll never be able to work for anyone else. On the other hand, if you aren't willing to tell yourself what to do and then do it, I'd advise you not to try to work out of your home.

Every year, new businesses fail. This is due to a variety of causes, but one reason is that many people don't realize how challenging it is to work unsupervised. I've seen very capable people unravel after a few months of working at home. Once they get back into a corporate environment, where they are stimulated by the presence of a boss and co-workers and have help and support from others, they are not only happier but much more effective.

Setting your own hours

Advantage: *No time clock to punch.*

Challenge: *No regular schedule.*

Good time management is crucial for the home office professional. Not only are you juggling all of those roles I mentioned earlier, you are undoubtedly finding plenty of things to do around the house other than professional work. Often what should be a two-hour project can end up taking 48 hours to complete. Working your own hours at your own pace is fine, until the amount of work you produce drops. By disciplining yourself and getting on a regular schedule, you can still be productive while enjoying the benefits of working at home.

Self-employed home office professionals have the satisfaction of running their own business and watching it grow through the results of their own efforts. They also bear full responsibility for all of the problems, deadlines, and bills. If you're not on someone else's payroll, time truly is money. Each interruption and wasted hour translates into less work accomplished and less income. Some relatively simple changes in the way you run your home office can save you an enormous amount of time, which translates into greater success.

Many home office professionals value their freedom to work odd hours, particularly at night or on weekends, when interruptions are few. If you don't get as much done during the day as you'd hoped, you can always get in a few hours in the evening. For some people, the problem is knowing when to stop!

Working alone

Advantage: *No need to worry about office politics or irritating co-workers.*

Challenge: *Feeling isolated, "out of the loop," and even lonely.*

If you have a social nature, be sure to find or create opportunities for face-to-face conversation or you may end up resenting your work and looking for ways to get away from your home office.

When one of my clients, Bev, started a special event company, she was excited about her new business. However, as the months passed she became less and less motivated. Bev missed talking with friends and co-workers in person, and she wasn't enjoying her new lifestyle as much as she thought she would. I suggested that Bev start a local support network made up of other entrepreneurs and home office professionals. She did, and now they meet every two weeks to socialize and share ideas.

Seeing clients at home

Advantage: *You don't waste time traveling to clients or waiting for them to show up.*

Challenge: *Clients see how you live and work.*

If your home office is in, say, a separate wing of the house with a separate entrance, you don't have to worry about clients seeing your laundry or your family's mess. If your office is in a living area of your home, however, you need to think about ways to avoid the need

> Depending upon how tidy you are and where your workspace is located, having clients come to your home can be stressful and possibly embarrassing.

for last-minute cleaning sessions before clients show up. You may find it helpful to use a folding screen, or French doors with curtained panels, or other devices that set your office apart from the rest of the house, draw attention to your workspace, and hide the rest of your home from view.

In a corporate environment, there are a lot of desks, and none are particularly interesting. In a home office, your desk is the center of attention, and it says something about you. Getting and keeping it organized will help you make a professional impression when clients come to your home.

No dress code

Advantage: *You can work in sweat pants if you feel like it.*

Challenge: *You have to try harder to achieve a professional appearance when necessary.*

I know a graphics designer who works at home who actually puts on a business suit and high heels before making her business calls. This helps her feel professional while she's tackling a difficult call. After she's off the phone, however, she takes off her heels and gets back to work in comfort.

As "dressing for success" shows, clothes are more than just pieces of material you happen to have on your body. A professional appearance can help you feel more capable, just as casual clothes can, at times, make you feel at a disadvantage even if no one is looking at you.

Some people are more sensitive to this issue than others, depending upon their line of work and other factors. My usual advice to clients is to dress comfortably (which to some may mean business attire) while you're working at home and switch to business attire when meeting with clients.

No commuting

Advantage: *You save time, energy, and money.*

Challenge: *You can't escape your work.*

For convenience, walking 20 steps to your office can't be beat. Whenever I'm stuck in traffic I realize how glad I am that I work at home and generally can avoid being trapped in an unmoving car. On the other hand, when you work at home your job is always present, physically and psychologically.

If you can close the door on your home office, you're lucky. Some home office professionals who don't have a spare room to use as an office design a workspace that closes up when not in use. This way their job is less intrusive when they are entertaining or spending time with their family.

Merging your personal and professional lives

Advantage: *You can take time during the day for personal calls, errands, and other tasks.*

Challenge: *Trying to juggle both personal and professional obligations at the same time.*

When you work in a corporate office, it's understood that you leave your personal life behind as much as possible. When you work at home, however, there is no escaping your personal life, whether it's last night's dishes, phone calls, bills, the dog, the kids, or all of these. To keep from becoming overwhelmed by personal obligations, try the following:

- Set up your home office in a quiet part of the house where you won't be interrupted. If at all possible, claim a spare room.

- Install a separate phone line for your business, and put voice mail or some other type of answering system on both lines.

- Ignore any personal tasks that aren't essential. Otherwise, you could easily spend all day housecleaning instead of working.

- Put off any personal tasks you can accomplish after hours, such as picking up dry cleaning, buying groceries, or making personal calls.

- Put the remaining essential personal tasks on your To-Do list, along with your business obligations, under separate headings.

One of the unique challenges of a home office is that you need to be able to accommodate both your personal and professional records. Although one of my home-based clients has a separate "bill-paying desk," most home office professionals need to find ways to combine the storage of their work files and their home files, such as insurance policies, investment information, tax returns, and product information.

QUICK TIP FOR HOME OFFICE PROFESSIONALS

Don't try to keep your personal and professional lives completely separate. Home office professionals need to find ways to combine their work obligations with their personal tasks in a way that sacrifices neither. It might surprise you to hear that the key to doing this successfully is not to try to completely separate your personal and professional lives. I've found that this is not only futile, it's inefficient. As you plan your day or your week, write down any personal tasks you need to accomplish, but list them separately from your business tasks. This way you can focus on work-related tasks without losing track of personal obligations.

Several of my home office clients, including both moms and dads, work at home so that one parent can be near the children while the other parent goes off to a corporate office. Paul and Leah feel strongly that one of them should be around for the children, so when Paul was laid off from his corporate job, Leah went back to work and Paul set up a consulting business at home. Although a babysitter comes to the house every day, Paul still finds that he gets interrupted by the kids, as well as called upon to deal with unexpected events. When these situations are important—for example, when their daughter Zoe needed stitches—Paul is particularly glad that he's immediately available. However, interruptions over trivial matters take up his time unnecessarily, break his concentration, make him appear unprofessional, and raise his blood pressure.

Paul found that reading the riot act to the children and their sitter was minimally effective, so he called me for ideas. First, we moved his office into the basement. Although Paul initially didn't like the idea of being moved to the "dungeon," he discovered that the benefits of being out of sight, behind a closed door, outweighed the disadvantages of working below ground. Next we set up a two-way intercom system so that Paul could stay in touch with his family without having to leave his office for every small question. He also takes breaks throughout the day to eat lunch with his kids and play with them for a few minutes. We also reserved a drawer in his desk for toys that are brought out only in desperate circumstances, such as when he has to make a business call with a child on his lap. (He hasn't had to use the drawer yet, but likes knowing that the diversion is there just in case.) Paul still finds it challenging to work with children in the house, but he also deeply values the close relationship he now has with his kids.

Letting people know you mean business

One of my clients who works at home takes time off every afternoon for a long walk. He finds this energizes him and clears his mind for another four hours of work. After he missed his walk for a week, a neighbor stopped him on the street and asked, "Say, did you find a job?"

Some people believe that if you work at home, you don't have a "real" job and you can't be serious about what you do. Some corporate employees are suspicious of work that doesn't originate in an office building. Obviously these people are missing the point, but their attitude presents a problem for you. To overcome these types of preconceived ideas, people who work at home have to try extra hard to be professional. With that in mind, I recommend that you do the following:

- Maintain normal business hours as much as possible.
- Keep your office businesslike, especially if clients will be seeing it.
- Avoid talking to clients at times when dogs or children might interrupt you.
- Spend the necessary money on quality stationery, marketing materials, and a printer.
- Consider using a post office box or mail services box for business mail.
- Be extra prompt, extra well prepared, and extra well groomed when you need to be.
- Project confidence.

If you believe in yourself, others will believe in you, too.

Finding the Right Place for Your Home Office

2

Finding the Right Place for Your Home Office

It's important to carefully evaluate every room in your home before deciding where your office should be. Even if you have already set up a home office, this is still a useful exercise. There may be a better place for it. Answering the following questions about each space you might use will help you find the ideal location for your home office:

- Will you actually work in this area?

- Will distractions be kept to a minimum?

- Is there (or could there be) ample lighting?

- How difficult would it be to run phone lines into this space?

- Are there enough electrical outlets?

- Could you set up an Internet connection?

- Is this space comfortable year-round?

- Is there room for everything you need (desk, file cabinet, computer, and so on)?

- Is there room for you to display samples of your work (if needed)?

- Is there enough storage space? Or is there room for storage nearby?

If clients will be coming to your home, also consider the following:

- Can you meet with clients comfortably in this space?
- Is there a separate entrance for clients to use?
- Is there a way to keep clients from seeing the rest of your home?

If possible, have clients use a separate entrance, or locate your office near an entrance. Even though your office may be

> The only part of your home that clients should see is your office.

organized and your presentation professional, you send an entirely different message if you take your clients on a tour through a home that is disorganized.

Unless you do everything yourself, remodeling is expensive. You may have to spend some money fixing up the right spot for your office. For example, you might want phone lines installed or have an electrician put in good lighting or electric heat. Try to think long term. It's better to invest in the right location now than to settle for a space that costs less but will no longer suit your needs in a year or two. If there is any way to avoid it, you don't want to go through the aggravation of moving your office later.

An extra room is the ideal place for a home office, but not everyone has the space. If you don't have a room to spare, the next best choice is to use a portion of an out-of-the-way room such as a guest room or your bedroom. You can also set up a home office within your living room, dining room, family room, or kitchen. Some people successfully convert their basement, garage, or even a closet into a functional workspace. I've seen people make amazing transformations, turning awkward and inconvenient spaces into organized, efficient, comfortable offices.

Some space-saving tricks

As you consider your options, keep in mind that you don't necessarily need to set up a traditional office with a big, executive-style desk and an oversized credenza. These days there are many innovative products on the market, some geared specifically to home office professionals, that allow you to be more flexible in your choices.

If you plan to set up your home office in a living area, for example, in your living room, dining room, or guest room, consider using a rolling computer work station and a rolling file cart. Modular furniture makes is easy to move your office around. When you entertain, all you have to do is push your office furniture against the wall or into another room.

A computer armoire gives you room to store your computer and office equipment and closes at the end of the day. (Courtesy of Crate & Barrel, photo ©Steven McDonald)

There are a variety of computer carts or computer work stations available. When searching for one, consider the following questions. Is it big enough for your computer system? If you have two printers or a large printer, you may need more room. Do you have enough room to work? If you like to spread your papers on your desk, you may require more space. Do you want to hide your computer when it's not in use? Use a computer cart with a top that folds or rolls down and locks. Another option is to use an armoire specifically designed to hold computer equipment.

Before you buy any type of computer furniture make sure each piece is sturdy, well built and will last. Also, make sure it will fit through the door, up a staircase or within a hallway.

Sample layouts

Included in the following pages are some sample layouts showing how you might meet the challenge of finding a place at home for your office. Each layout includes some or all of the following basic home office essentials:

- Desk
- Chair
- Shelves
- File cabinet
- Fax
- Computer
- Printer
- Computer workstation

Exactly how you lay out your office depends upon many factors, including the size and shape of the space that's available and the type of furniture and equipment you choose. As you read this book, you'll make many decisions that will affect your workspace. You'll also find the right location for many smaller items—for example, your phone, answering machine (if you're not using a voice mail system), and various office organizing products that aren't pictured here. These layouts are intended to help you think about the various options your home provides.

The spare room

Advantage: *The perfect solution, if you have the space.*

Disadvantage: *None.*

Having an entire room to devote to your office is the ideal situation. You have plenty of space in which to consolidate everything related to your job, you can work in privacy, distractions are minimized, and you don't have to worry about

A separate office is the most professional place in which to meet clients.

putting all of your papers away when guests come over. At the end of the day you can close the door behind you and enjoy the rest of your home.

Before you cross this option off your list, consider whether or not you have a seldom-used room—for example, a dining room, that could be converted into an office. Attic or loft spaces are other possibilities to think about.

If you have the luxury of converting a spare room into an office, do an absolutely thorough job of it. Take the seasonal clothing out of the closet and remove any hobby equipment you're storing there. Limit everything in the room to work-related items, and use this room only for working. These elements are vital for taking a home office deduction.

The guest bedroom

Advantage: *Almost as good as setting up your office in a spare room.*

Disadvantage: *Inconvenient when guests actually visit.*

While it is extremely helpful to have your office in a separate, out-of-the-way room that has a door, rearranging a guest bedroom so that it can accommodate your home office is definitely better than having your office in a portion of a room with more traffic, such as a family room.

In order to have your guest room double as your office (or is it vice versa?) you may have to invest in a hideaway bed. A less expensive option is a futon.

If you need to keep your guest bedroom relatively intact, for example, maybe you have regular visitors who need access to a bed, a dresser, and some shelves, designate a corner of the room as your office. You might reserve a drawer or two of the dresser for office supplies. One of my clients used folding screens to surround her work area. When she stepped behind them and sat at her desk, she was ready to work, and her guests didn't feel they were intruding on her private workspace. Another option is to use a computer armoire.

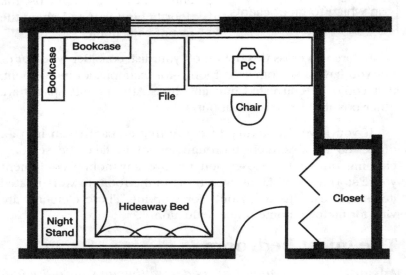

How to set up an office in a guest bedroom. Note: In this office, a computer cart holds both a computer (on top) and a printer and CPU(underneath). With this arrangement, you would need blinds or curtains in the window to cut down on glare.

Your bedroom

Advantage: *It's good to have your office in a separate room, even if it has to be your bedroom.*

Disadvantage: *Sleeping with your work.*

I usually advise clients not to put their home office in their bedroom if there is any way to avoid it. However, if you have to choose between setting up your office in your bedroom or in a portion of another living area in your home in which you will have absolutely no privacy,

> With a little ingenuity, you can design a workspace that closes up or is hidden from view after hours, allowing you to sleep in peace.

choose the bedroom. The advantages of working in a separate room without constant interruptions outweigh the inconveniences of sleeping with your job.

When your office is in your bedroom, you'll probably have only limited storage space, so you'll need to think about other areas in which to store your work-related materials. If clients will be coming to your home, you'll probably want to clean up the dining room and meet with them there.

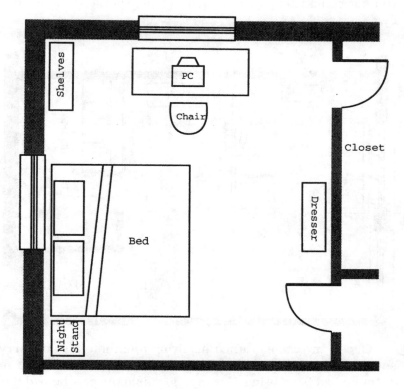

The living room, dining room, or family room

Advantage: *You have plenty of room in which to spread out your papers while you work.*

Disadvantage: *In a living area, it's difficult to keep your personal life from intruding on your work.*

When your office is in a corner of a living area of your home, there is constant friction between your work life and your personal life. If you live quietly by yourself, or if the area you choose is seldom used, the inconveniences are certainly manageable (for example, having to clean up before entertaining). However, if you live with others, you can expect their need to use this shared living space to conflict with your needs. You may be interrupted often, your paperwork is at risk when others have access to your desk, and it's more difficult to concentrate when you're surrounded by other people's clutter (not to mention your own).

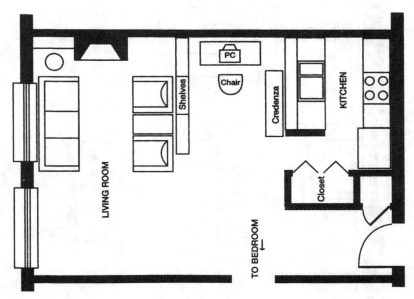

One of my clients turned his living room into a studio very successfully. He found it served his needs better than the spare room he had been using. However, for the most part he had this territory to himself. During the day he was alone in the house, and his wife seldom ventured into the living room unless they were entertaining.

If you live in a one-bedroom apartment and can't set up your office in your bedroom, you have to create a workspace in the living area of your apartment. You may have to sacrifice having a separate dining area. Use high shelves to separate your workspace from the rest of your apartment.

The kitchen

Advantage: *You can stay in contact with your family.*

Disadvantage: *You are in constant contact with your family.*

If you have a kitchen big enough to accommodate a home office, you may also have a big family to go along with it, making your kitchen the "Grand Central Station" of your home. If your kitchen sees a lot of traffic, expect constant interruptions, clutter, and distractions. If you use the kitchen table as a work area, you'll constantly shuffle your papers from place to place. However, some people prefer working in their kitchen because they feel comfortable there.

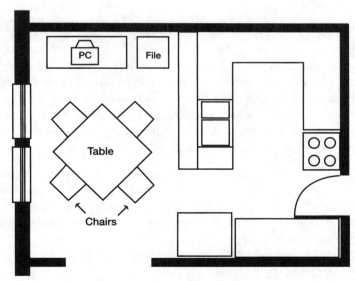

How to set up an office in your kitchen. Note: With this arrangement, shelves or cabinets could be mounted on the wall above the desk.

If you set up your office in the kitchen, make sure you have a clear area in which to work and a place to put a two-drawer file cabinet (if you don't have a built-in work area). You could even put a piece of fabric over your file cabinet when you're not working so that it blends in with its surroundings.

The basement

Advantage: *An out-of-the-way place in which to work.*

Disadvantage: *Can be depressing: dark, damp, and/or lonely.*

> A basement office has all of the advantages of an office in a separate room, including privacy, few distractions, and a single area in which to put all of your work-related items.

If you can transform your basement (or, more likely, a portion of your basement) into a brightly lit, comfortable work area, this is a good option for you. On the other hand, if you like to be near windows while you work, or if your basement is damp, musty, or smells of furnace fumes, look elsewhere.

Brenda, a district manager for a line of cosmetics, called me because she was struggling daily to find enough time to fill orders, call her sales reps, and meet with clients. When I went to Brenda's home to consult with her, it was obvious that her biggest problem was the lack of a regular place in which to work. Some days she worked in her bedroom. Other days she used the kitchen table.

We developed a plan for turning Brenda's basement into a home office. She had the walls covered with sheet rock and painted white. Then she added carpeting, track lighting, and built-in shelves. Her new office has changed the way she works, as well as the way she feels about her work.

The garage

Advantage: *Working in an area separated from the rest of your home, and thus more private.*

Disadvantage: *Losing the use of your garage for other purposes.*

By remodeling your garage into a home office, you can create a quiet, private workspace that is completely set off from the rest of the house. The downside of creating a garage office is that the remodeling can be expensive and you may miss being able to use that space for parking your car and storing your lawn mower. Depending upon how big your garage is, you might remodel part of it and share it with your car.

One of my clients, a bookkeeper, liked the freedom of working at home, yet wanted to keep her office and her home separate. She used to have her office in a spare bedroom, but she found she couldn't walk past the door without going in and doing some work.

> A garage is a good alternative for you if you want to work at home but still want the feeling of "going to the office" each day.

To satisfy her needs, she converted her garage into an office. She added insulation and a window so that she could use a window air-conditioning unit in the summer and a space heater in the winter. When she went to work she would leave through the front door of her house and enter her office through a side door in her garage. By physically separating her office from her home, she was able to have the feeling of working outside her home without having to commute.

Closets

Advantage: *A compact office behind closed doors.*

Disadvantages: *Limited space, and the loss of the use of your closet for storage.*

A large closet can be converted into a nice little work area. You'll need to install some overhead shelves for storage, at least one phone line, a flat surface for your desktop, lighting above and shelves or drawers below, and a file cabinet next to (or under) your work surface. If your closet has sliding doors, you'll need to change them into regular doors so that both can be open while you work. Another option is to fully open up the length of the closet and install folding accordion-style doors.

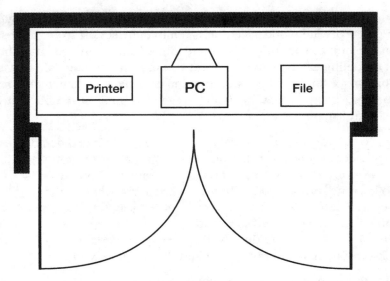

How to set up a closet office. Note: This arrangement requires a closet space at least three feet deep and nine feet long. The chair could be stored either under the desk or outside the closet when not in use. Shelves or cabinets could be placed above the desk.

Hallways, alcoves, landings, and under stairs

Consider all areas of your home, including wide hallways, alcoves and landings as places for your home office. Again, keep in mind whether these are high-traffic areas or too secluded to allow you to work.

Clearing out your chosen office space

Now that you've decided where you are going to set up your office, you have to go through your office-to-be and remove the things that don't belong there. Many people find it easier to store something than to make the decision to keep it or to throw it away. Use this opportunity to move items you no longer need right out of the house, rather than rearrange junk.

Getting rid of possessions can be difficult. Some people feel they are throwing away a part of themselves or their history when they get rid of something. Others hate to get rid of something that is in perfectly good shape or that seems as if it might be useful someday.

The biggest problem with being a pack rat is that you accumulate too much clutter. Eventually clutter interferes with your efficiency, not only because you run out of places to store everything, but because you get so absorbed in "making do" with items you already have that you may miss valuable new opportunities. You also end up wasting time and energy resurrecting or wearing out old items, or searching for the items you need, when it's actually far simpler and even cheaper to buy exactly what you need when you need it.

> When you keep too many things, eventually you lose track of what you have and where everything is.

As we're clearing out their desks, clients of mine often say, "I've been looking for that," or, "I didn't even know I had that!" The things you really do need can get buried under the extra items you would be better off without.

You may be afraid that the minute you throw something away, you'll need it. Everyone has experienced this phenomenon. However, what you have to realize is that before you got rid of those old ice skates, or your books from college, or your baseball trophy from high school, chances are you had either forgotten you had it or forgotten where it was. Either way, it actually wasn't of any use to you. When you keep only those things you need, you'll know what you have and where everything is, and the useful items won't get buried under the items you don't need.

James, a researcher, needed help decluttering a spare bedroom before he could use it as a home office. When I walked into the room, there were boxes stacked in the closet and against the wall. He told me he had recently moved in and hadn't had time to unpack them. When I discovered that in fact he'd been living in his home for two years, the decluttering job suddenly got easier. Anything you don't even look at for two years can probably be safely thrown out, donated, or sold.

QUICK TIP FOR HOME OFFICE PROFESSIONALS

The "Toss or Keep?" Test. There are three questions to ask yourself to determine whether or not you should keep something.

1) Have I used this item within the past year?

2) Is it serving a specific purpose?

3) Do I have a place to store it where I can find it again?

If you answered no to any of these questions, consider giving or throwing the item away. If you decide to keep it, make sure you can find it when you need it!

A step-by-step plan for decluttering

Cleaning out your chosen office space will take time. How long it will take depends upon the size of the space, the amount of stuff you have there already, and how long you've been accumulating things in this space. If possible, schedule enough time to work on this project without interruption until it is completed. If you have to stop in the middle, you may not be able to finish for another week. This means you'll spend a week stepping over all of the things you're trying to organize, and you may end up pushing all of the clutter back into your office space again. If you're unable to block out enough time to finish the project or know that it will take more than one day, set aside time during the week to clear out the room section by section. The following are recommendations for clearing out your chosen space.

1) Take out any large items (furniture, skis, exercise machines, luggage, and so on) that don't belong in your office and put them elsewhere. Some people keep a television set in their office for work-related viewing, but most people are better off without one around.

2) Get four large bags in which to place the remaining smaller items. The point of using the bags is to keep you focused on your office. If you have to leave to put an item away, you may get sidetracked. Label the bags respectively as follows:

   • **Give away** (charity items)

- **Put away** (items that belong in other rooms in your home)
- **Storage**
- **Trash**

3) Work systematically. Start by decluttering one corner of your office area and work your way around the room. It's important to focus on just one section at a time. I've found that a clockwise approach works best and reduces the tendency to jump from section to section.

4) Go back to the large items. Use the system you used for the smaller items: give them away, put them elsewhere in your home, put them in storage, or throw them out.

This is a big decluttering project, but if it's done correctly, you should never have to do it again, especially to this degree. Although things will look terrible when your office space is in transition, don't get discouraged. The end result will be well worth the time you spend.

QUICK TIP FOR HOME OFFICE PROFESSIONALS

When you're cleaning up, try to decide quickly what to do with each item. Don't put off making up your mind, because delaying doesn't make the process any easier. Avoid making a "decide later" pile. As you begin to get tired, everything will end up in that pile, and nothing will get thrown out!

Staying decluttered

To keep your office decluttered in the future, I recommend the following:

- Don't bring anything into your work area without first asking yourself if you really need it.

- Keep only work-related items in your office.

- Whenever an item breaks, whether it's an expensive pen or a printer, get it fixed within a week or get rid of it.

One of the best ways to keep your office uncluttered is to set up organizing systems that help you process your paperwork efficiently. In the next chapter, we'll start with a basic—how to arrange your workspace.

Arranging Your Workspace

3

Arranging Your Workspace

Your home office can be as basic or as elaborate as you want, but the way it is laid out will affect your productivity. The key is to make it work for you. It has to be a place you enjoy, and it has to be organized in a way that both suits your working style and meets your business needs efficiently.

Organizing from the ground up

Organizing your workspace to suit your needs is the first step to taking control of your home office. Once you start thinking in terms of greater efficiency, you are on your way to organizing every aspect of your business.

People have told me that they were born disorganized and will probably die disorganized. You don't have to be born organized in order to get organized. Getting organized requires what I call the four keys to organization: acknowledgment, desire, direction, and action.

1) **Acknowledgment.** First you have to admit that your home office needs to be organized. Even if in reality your office already works for you, you probably could make changes that would contribute to your greater productivity.

2) **Desire.** You won't alter your habits or your habitat unless you see a need and want to change. A motivating

---

idea that works for most people is the fact that organizing is the key to greater professional success.

3) **Direction.** Once you've acknowledged a need to change, professional advice is helpful in getting you started. Although organizing your home office is largely a matter of common sense, there are tricks, products, and systems of which you may be unaware. This book will give you the direction you need to implement changes.

4) **Action.** Good intentions alone won't get you organized. Now that you've located the best place for your home office, it's time to take action.

Where to begin

Here's a game plan for setting up your own personalized workspace. Developing exactly the right layout for you will take time, so please don't try to rush through these steps. The more thought you put into your office layout up front, the fewer adjustments you'll need to make later.

- **Write down your needs.** Do you need an office that will comfortably accommodate clients? Do you need space for samples, or forms, or reference books? Do you need special shelves or flat files for watercolor paper or architectural renderings? Do you need to fit in a drafting table or a large, open surface for cutting fabric or laying out paperwork? How would you arrange your ideal office and what would you put in it?

- **Consider your options.** In this chapter you'll find three basic sample layouts to think about. Most offices roughly follow one of these arrangements, but the possibilities are endless. What are the advantages and limitations of your chosen space?

- **Think about furniture.** What do you have on hand, and what do you need to buy? Maybe you can raid a table or desk or chair from another part of the house. (Warning: if existing furniture doesn't quite suit your needs, don't try to make do with it. It will only cause you irritation.) Furniture manufacturers have finally realized the need for affordable, good quality furniture for home offices and are now making it available.

- **Read the rest of this book for ideas.** You may find that there's a product you weren't aware of, or a way of handling paperwork that requires a certain type of file cabinet, or a way to use your wall space to your advantage. Before you make up your mind about how you want to arrange your workspace, review the organizational methods that will best work for you.

- **Plan your office on a grid.** It's a good idea to measure your office space, draw it on a grid, and then fit in any furniture you plan to use. To make the best use of your space, you may discover that you need to go out and buy a desk or table that is exactly 40 inches long—not 38, and not 42. Playing around with various arrangements on a paper grid beats wrestling with actual furniture, and you can think more clearly when you aren't surrounded by office equipment. There are computer programs available that give you a virtual layout of your home and home office. Unless you're remodeling or building a home, these design programs are probably more than you need. An alternative to a computer program is a paper-based product that has pre-cut furniture and can be customized to simulate your office.

- **Shop for what you need.** Bring your grid as well as a list of what you need to buy, with exact dimensions. The fewer surprises you have at the end of this process, the better. Like dessert, the best part comes last. After you've been through all of these steps, you'll be ready to move in.

QUICK TIP FOR HOME OFFICE PROFESSIONALS

It's never too late to change. If you want to get organized, you can. If you want to improve, you can. People have different reasons—personal, professional, psychological—for wanting to get organized. Some people realize they are overwhelmed and want to reduce their stress level. Others are ashamed of themselves for being disorganized. Many people would like to have more free time, and everyone would like to have more money. Keep your personal motivation in mind as you implement new organizational strategies.

Choosing a basic layout

Take a look at the three basic layouts that follow and see which appeals to you and might work in your available space. Keep in mind that this is only a first step. In later chapters you'll be refining your workspace so that it is fully customized to suit your needs. The following layouts include some or all of the same office essentials as the layouts in Chapter 2:

- Desk
- Computer workstation
- Chair
- Shelves
- File cabinet
- Fax
- Personal Computer (PC) or MS Windows operated computers
- Printer

If you have other sizable office equipment, for example, a copier, drafting table, credenza or floor lamp, start thinking about how they might fit into your overall design. Save space by putting your CPU under your desk or computer workstation.

The U-shaped work area

This arrangement is ideal because it allows you to keep everything within reach on three surfaces. In a U-shaped arrangement, to the left of your desk you might have a computer cart that houses all of your electronic equipment. To the right you might have a credenza, table or horizontal file cabinet with a fax machine and a phone/answering machine. A stand-alone phone could be placed on your desk, if you don't want to use your fax phone or if you have a separate line for business—a good idea by the way. This layout is extremely convenient. All you have to do is swivel your chair one way or the other while you work. The only disadvantage to this arrangement is that it requires more space than an L-shaped arrangement, provided that there is only one entry and exit in the room and the windows won't be blocked by furniture. Another disadvantage is that if your desk is too long, or the return is on a side that would block a door or window, you may have to place it against the wall (not optimal for seeing clients).

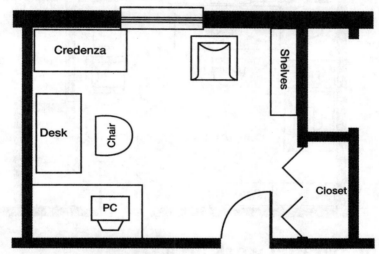

The L-shaped work area

The L-shaped work area offers the important advantage of getting equipment off your desk and onto a secondary surface. For example, on a computer stand perpendicular to your desk (or credenza that you could use as a writing surface), you could place your monitor, keyboard, printer and fax and place your CPU underneath. Unless your credenza doubles as a computer stand, you wouldn't have legroom underneath the credenza, yet you could still write by swiveling slightly to your credenza. The advantage of a credenza over a desk is more file drawers. Your phone, office supplies that you use often (tape dispenser, stapler, pen and pencil holder, etc.) would be on top of your desk or in a nearby desk drawer, leaving your desk relatively clear for work in progress. The only disadvantage to the L-shape, compared to the U-shape, is lack of an additional open space to work. If you have the room, you may consider adding an extra surface to create a U-shape. If you would tend to use the extra surface to store unnecessary items that would only serve to clutter your workspace and distract you, then you should stick with the L-shape.

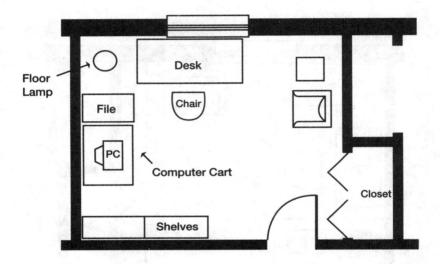

The parallel work area

With this layout, your desk faces into the room and your secondary surface is behind you. Although the two surfaces aren't next to each other, you can easily access everything you need. One surface could be your computer desk or table that holds all of your computer equipment and fax, and the other desk could hold your phone, files and supplies you use daily or weekly. Another option is a traditional desk that holds the items you use often and the other secondary surface a credenza (either a standard credenza or one that doubles as a computer stand). The same disadvantage as the L-shape applies to the parallel arrangement. Make sure that the two surfaces will give you enough surface room to work.

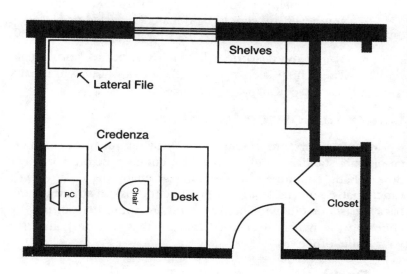

Refining your master plan

As you think about how to arrange your workspace, keep in mind the following general office-organizing guidelines:

- **Keep related items near one another.** For example, arrange your computer and printer so they are next to each other, and put your computer reference books on a shelf above them. Store all of your paper—printer paper, fax paper, legal pads (whatever you use) in the same place.

- **Keep the items you use often close at hand.** The things you need constantly should be within reach. Items you use occasionally should go in drawers or in a closet in your home office. Work-related items you seldom use or files you rarely refer to should be boxed up and stored on pallets in your garage and basement, or if you have the room and cabinet to spare, in a file cabinet. As a last resort, store this seldom-used information in another room. Store it together, and limit it to one other room. When you start stashing it around your home, you'll forget that you own it. Finally, items you never use should be donated, recycled or placed in your next garage sale.

• **You'll need some files in or next to your desk.** These help keep papers off your desk but within easy reach (see Chapter 5 for ideas).

Choosing office furniture

Manufacturers are constantly improving furniture to meet ergonomic standards and our need for comfort. Before you buy a desk, chair, computer workstation or chair, make sure it is functional, comfortable and will reduce the risk of straining your back, wrists or elbows. The following are some helpful tips for choosing the major pieces of furniture that will be going into your home office.

Desks

• If you like to tuck things away, buy a desk with only a few drawers. You'll just end up stuffing things in them.

• If you're not a pack rat, buy a desk that has enough drawer space to hold your everyday items. This will help keep your desktop clear. A desk file drawer is also helpful for keeping papers you are currently working on nearby but out of sight.

• Think vertically and purchase furniture that holds a computer, keyboard, CPU, and printer. If there's no place for a CPU, use a holder that stores your CPU in its side under your desk. An armoire is a space-saving piece of furniture that allows you to keep all of your equipment in one place.

• If you have a limited amount of workspace available, use a printer stand to hold your printer and paper and keyboard extender or monitor stand if you don't have a keyboard drawer.

Gene, a retired accountant, purchased the desk he had used for twenty years in his corporate job and brought it to his home office. After a few months, he started to regret ever having bought it. It had served him well in his corporate job, but it was too large for his home office. Also, it had no file drawer, something he needed now that he no longer had access to the large file cabinets he'd had at work. Gene ended up selling his old desk and buying a smaller desk with file space.

A computer workstation gives you places to store your equipment and leaves you room to work. (Courtesy of Computer Furniture Direct)

Chairs

If your current office chair is part of your dining room set, replace it immediately. If you don't, your back will let you know that you've made a big mistake. An office chair should support your back, not interfere with the movement of your arms, and absorb and distribute your weight. A few other factors to consider when buying a chair are:

- *Lumbar support* to reduce the strain on your lower back.

- *Waterfall seat.* The front edge of the seat is rounded to prevent restricted circulation and compression of nerves behind your knees.

- *Seat height and back height adjustments.*

- *Tilt mechanisms and tilt lock* to reduce strain and fatigue of your leg muscles.

- *Tension control.* Reclining tension that adjusts to your body weight for easier reclining.

File cabinets

Depending upon your filing needs and budget, you may want to consider options other than the traditional two- or four-drawer file cabinet. There are various factors you need to keep in mind:

- How much money do you want to spend?

- How much room do you have in your office?

- How much paperwork do you have?

- What future filing needs do you anticipate?

The following are some file storage options:

The traditional two- or four-drawer vertical file cabinet. If you choose one of these, make sure you get a sturdy one. What may seem to be a bargain on a low-quality cabinet may cost you more in the long run when you have to struggle to open and close the drawers, if the drawer falls on your foot, if you have to replace the handles, or if the entire thing gives out. Some file cabinets are deeper than others, so keep your office space in mind as you shop.

Lateral file cabinets hold your folders sideways instead of front to back. They take up more space horizontally, but have less depth. One of the nice benefits of a lateral file is that it provides a secondary work surface on top. You can place the files inside either facing you (front to back, which will leave additional room in the drawers for other things, i.e. supplies) or the traditional way, side to side.

Open-front files are specialized files most commonly seen in medical offices where there is constant retrieval and refiling of individual files. They do not accommodate hanging folders, and require special file folders that allow you to easily read the label on each folder.

Open file carts are most often used for work in progress (see page 85). However, if you have a limited amount of space in your office and a limited number of files, a file cart would work for you. One disadvantage of the open file cart is that its contents are visible to anyone who walks into your office.

File crates with file rods inside will hold a large number of hanging folders. They come in both rigid and collapsible types.

Open file crates, similar to milk crates, can be used either on a flat surface, open at the top, or stacked vertically, laid on their sides. If you use a file crate open at the top, you insert hanging folders so that they hook over the edges of the crate. If you use the crates with the open side facing out, you would use accordion files or file jackets to hold your papers. One of my clients, the owner of a home-based talent agency, used wire stacking crates with expanding folders to hold all of the video and audio tapes she constantly received.

"Milk crate" filing crates hold hanging folders and fit in just about anywhere. (Courtesy of Esselte Corporation)

Cardboard file boxes with lids are appropriate for files you need to store long term but to which you seldom refer.

If you have extremely valuable papers you wish to file at home, instead of in a safe deposit box, consider investing in a fireproof file box or file cabinet. If you're a pack rat, don't go overboard with file cabinets. You'll only find a way to fill them up.

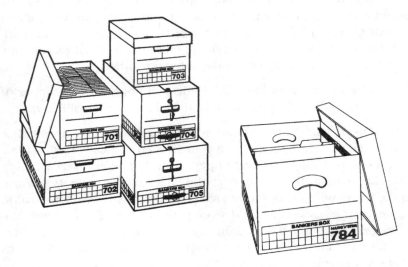

Bankers boxes, ideal for storing older reference files, are affordable on any budget. (Courtesy of Fellowes)

Other factors to consider in a home office:

- Invest in at least one bookcase to hold your resource materials, including computer manuals. Don't clutter your desk or credenza with books you rarely refer to. Another option is to add shelves within your office closet (if you have one) and store your books on the shelves.

- Don't forget about lighting. If you start to fade earlier and earlier each day, maybe it's due to poor lighting, a quick-fix that can affect your fatigue factor.

Multifunction peripherals

You can save space by buying a machine that does more than one job, for example, a fax-copier, or printer/scanner. Check the quality of these machines carefully. In some cases, you will be sacrificing the capability of one feature in order to include another. (See more about multifunctional peripherals in Chapter 13.)

A rolling storage system with drawers gives you room to hold supplies, files or both. (Courtesy of Iris)

Cheap tricks

Creating an efficient home office doesn't have to cost a fortune. The following tips are for you if you're interested in saving money:

- Turn an antique buffet, dresser or other piece of furniture into office supply storage.

- Instead of buying new bookshelves, add shelves in your closet to store samples, supplies or books. Create storage space in your closet for small office supplies by hanging a clear plastic shoe holder.

- Use wire shelves to hold your fax, printer or extra paper.

- Use a rolling storage system with drawers to store supplies, files or sales materials. You could place a smaller system in your closet to hold backup supplies.

- Place a laminate top, thick sheet of glass or long board across two file cabinets to create a work surface with storage space below.

Arranging your office furniture

Keep the following pointers in mind as you lay out your office:

- In a home office, it's not necessary to make your desk face out or face the door unless clients come to your home.

- If possible, don't put your computer in front of a window. The glare will be hard on your eyes. Make sure your computer screen is either facing a wall without a window or at an angle to a window, instead of in front of it, for better viewing. If you have to place your computer in front of a window, make sure you have curtains or blinds to block the outside light while you're looking at your monitor.

- Don't put your fax machine in a location where incoming documents might get lost. I have one client who was unaware that fax transmissions were piling up behind her file cabinet!

- Don't forget to allow space for opening file cabinet drawers—about an additional 24 inches. The cabinet itself may fit in a convenient space next to your shelves, but it's useless if you can't open the drawers all the way.

- If you have a hideaway bed in your office, make sure you leave enough room in front of it to open and close it easily, especially if you use it often. This way you'll cause less disruption to your office when you need to use the bed.

QUICK TIP FOR HOME OFFICE PROFESSIONALS

Don't try to organize everything in one day. It took awhile to get to the level of disorganization you now encounter. If you try to do everything at once, there's a high risk of getting discouraged and giving up altogether. Break the job down into manageable chunks, and tackle one thing at a time. Make a list of everything you'd like to accomplish, and reward yourself for each task completed. Scheduling several interruption-free afternoons is usually a more successful approach than trying to organize your entire business life in a day.

Using a planning grid

Some people avoid working with a planning grid because they can't draw. You really don't have to be able to draw to be able to push cutouts around on a piece of paper. Planning your office on paper is a valuable exercise because you may come up with some unexpected results that wouldn't have occurred to you if you were standing in the middle of your chosen space.

To use a planning grid, you'll need to make or buy graph paper with half-inch squares. On the grid, each one-half inch square corresponds to one foot of office space. You can use a finer grid if you wish, but probably half-inch squares are adequate.

Begin by drawing a rough aerial (bird's-eye view) of your office space on a piece of blank paper. Be sure to include any permanent fixtures, such as windows, doors, and radiators. (Don't block any vents if possible.)Then measure your office space exactly and draw a more precise layout on grid paper.

After your space is mapped out on the grid, you might want to run some copies of it in case you want to create a few versions. When you're ready to get serious, create to-scale cutouts of your office furniture and move them around on your grid. You don't need to go to the extreme of making computer and other technology cutouts, unless you want to be more precise.

You'll need symbols for office items such as the following:

- Desk
- Computer work station(s)
- Desk chair
- Credenza
- File cabinet
- Bookcase
- Chair(s) (for meetings or reading)
- Small conference table

To make the best possible use of your walls (see Chapter 5), you might consider drawing floor-to-ceiling elevated views of your wall space. First, draw anything permanent, such as wall switches or windows; then add any or all of the following:

- Bulletin board
- Shelves
- Wall clock

You may find that you want to add some stacking bins to your office, a rolling file cart, or some milk crates for storage. Before deciding on a final floor plan (and wall plan) for your office, I urge you to read on.

Buying and Storing Office Supplies

4

Buying and Storing Office Supplies

Office supplies are all of those small but essential items that enable you to work. Without pens and paper and files and envelopes, your home office would be useless.

Planning ahead and buying the right supplies will increase your productivity. You can waste unnecessary time fighting with a product that is the wrong one for your situation, so it's important to find products that meet your needs.

When you were in a corporate setting, you had access to more office supplies at no cost to you. When you work at home, and whether you own a business or are on an expense account, the cost of supplies matters.

The type of office supplies you buy or choose not to buy can make a difference in how effective you are. There are a few things to keep in mind about office supplies.

1) *You can't work without them.* If you've ever run out of ink for your printer in the middle of a job, you've experienced firsthand how one missing item can cause your entire workday to grind to a halt.

2) *Some products are specifically designed to keep you organized.* Many office products are designed for the sole purpose of helping you handle your paperwork and manage your time more efficiently, which translates into greater productivity.

3) *The right tools help you work faster.* A paper folder can help you get out a mailing quickly, a postal scale (or online postage) helps cut down on trips to the post office—even a staple remover saves you time.

4) *Some items help you look professional.* Printed stationery, for example, presents a polished image, which is especially important for a home office professional.

As a home-based professional, you need to be aware of the full range of office supplies available to you and how you can use them to best advantage. Moreover, because you don't have a corporate supply closet to raid when you run out of something, you need to set up a system that not only allows you to store an adequate supply of office products, but also lets you see at a glance when you're running low.

Chapter 3 discussed the larger items that belong in your home office, such as a desk, file cabinet, and electronic equipment. Now use the following lists to see how well equipped you are with the smaller items.

Basic home office supplies

One-time purchases

- Business card holder (either card file or notebook if contact information is not stored electronically)
- Calculator (if you don't use the one in your computer)
- Check endorsement stamp
- Clear shoeboxes to hold office supplies
- Computer disk, CD or Zip (or Jazz) holders
- Daily planner (or desk calendar or pocket calendar)
- Date stamp (if you want to track when information arrives)
- Drawer dividers (or trays)
- Hanging file frames for file cabinet (if not built in)
- Letter opener

- Stapler
- Staple remover
- Paper cutter
- Surge protector(s)
- Postal scale (may be leased—necessity depends upon how often you go to the post office)
- Clear tape and dispenser
- Ruler
- Three-hole punch
- Scissors
- Three-ring binders
- Vertical file holder
- Wastebasket

Supply items you'll need to replenish

- Address labels
- Sticky notes
- Business cards (yours, imprinted)
- CDs (for burning CDs)
- Clear tape
- Clear labels
- Computer disks
- Computer paper
- Copy paper (white, 20-lb., 8 1/2" by 11")
- Correction fluid (white, plus color to match letterhead)
- Hanging file folders (plus clear and colored plastic tabs and inserts)
- Highlighter markers
- Labels for file folders
- Legal pads
- Mailing labels

- Manila envelopes (9" x 12" and 10" x 13")
- File folders
- Note-size stationery (imprinted paper and envelopes)
- Overnight-delivery packing supplies (envelopes and labels)
- Paper clips
- Pencils
- Pens
- Printer cartridges
- Printer paper
- Rubber bands
- Stamps
- Staples
- Stationery (imprinted letterhead, plain second sheets, imprinted envelopes)

Add to this list any supplies that are specific to your business and delete those that do not apply. Then copy the list and refer to it whenever you're stocking up on office supplies. You could even keep a copy near your supply area (or closet), circling the items you need to buy on your next trip to the store.

> QUICK TIP FOR HOME OFFICE PROFESSIONALS
>
> Buy an extra set of office supplies for your family to use. Keep them stored in an area outside your office so that no one will raid your supplies.

Finding the right products for you

There are unused office products stashed in closets throughout the country. Do not buy anything that is just going to clutter up your workspace, no matter how appealing it seems.

Dave, a home-based psychologist, confessed to me after one of my seminars that he kept buying office-organizing products, thinking each new item would solve his problem with being disorganized. Instead, this created a new problem—lack of space in which to put all of the products he had bought.

I know many people periodically seized by an urge to get organized. They rush to the local office supply store and buy every product guaranteed to save them time, energy, and irritation. Then, mysteriously, their enthusiasm begins to decrease as their frustration with these products increases. Eventually they slip back into their old habits, convinced they will never be organized and feeling even worse than they did before. Instead of blaming the products, they blame themselves.

Similarly, I've seen people try to mimic their more organized friends by buying the same products and hoping to get the same results. When it comes to organizing, everyone

> The fact that a product works for someone else doesn't mean it will work for you.

has different needs, and these needs have to be met differently.

Companies devote endless hours to developing products to fit consumers' needs. They develop a product, work with focus groups, and refine the product based on the results of these groups. But even all of this effort does not ensure that a product is perfect or will work for you.

Instead of trying to adapt yourself to a product, whether it's a vertical file holder, drawer organizer or calendar, find a product that suits your needs. To do this, you must first identify the areas in which you're having organizational problems.

I can't tell you what to run out and buy, but I can show you some organizational methods that work for various personality types. After reading the rest of this book, you'll know exactly where you need to focus your energies. You may find that there's a filing system you should implement, or a daily planner that would solve your scheduling troubles. Once you know what you need, go out and find the right product for you. Then you will use it, it won't clutter up your office, and you will be organized.

QUICK TIP FOR HOME OFFICE PROFESSIONALS

Don't expect any product to organize you. Many people believe that a helpful product should automatically make them organized. A product can make organizing easier, but if you don't have basic skills in a certain area, the product won't help. Believing that an organizational product should get you organized is like expecting your car to drive you somewhere on its own. Carefully consider any product before you buy it and decide if it will indeed help you get organized or keep you from being organized.

Keeping costs down

Large corporations and small businesses alike waste hundreds, even thousands of dollars each year on unnecessary office supplies. A large corporation may not notice these extra dollars right away, but in a small business, every dollar counts. There are several ways you can keep office supply costs down.

1) **Always use a list when you go to the store.** A list keeps you from buying what you don't need and reminds you of what you do need to buy. Most people end up spending a little more than they expected every time they go to the store. By using a list, you'll remember to get everything you need, and you'll save money by making fewer trips to the store.

2) **Buy only what you need, in the quantity you need.** To reduce the amount of time you spend shopping, buy enough office supplies for at least two months. When you first start working in your home office, you won't know exactly how much to buy, but after awhile you'll develop a pattern and you'll know how long supplies will last.

3) **Don't buy more than you can efficiently store.** Buying large quantities of office supplies can be cost effective, but extra supplies won't save you money if they get ruined in the basement, if you forget you have them, or if you can't find them when you need them. If you can't immediately get your hands on a certain item, you'll probably go out and buy another, so you end up replacing what you've already got. Hint: many supplies are cheaper by the case. Consider splitting the cost with another home office professional.

4) **Before you buy anything on sale, make sure you need it.** As the saying goes, "If it's on sale, and you don't need it, it's not a bargain."

5) **Buy from discount office supply stores.** The prices at superstores are often much lower than those of traditional office supply stores.

6) **Buy quality.** Both quality and quantity count. Sometimes when you buy something that seems like a bargain, you end up getting what you paid for.

7) **Replenish your supplies before you run out.** Buying ahead of need gives you a chance to comparison shop and take advantage of sales. Also, running out at the last minute for a needed item is an inefficient use of time.

8) **Squeeze all the life you can out of your supplies.** For example, laser-printer cartridges can usually be cleaned out and refilled a few times before you need to buy a new cartridge.

Storing extra office supplies

If your home office has more than one user, it's vital that you keep all of your supplies—both your extra supplies and the everyday variety—labeled. If more than one person will be looking for the correction fluid, or a blank CD, or a fresh ream of copy paper, label where everything goes so that all hands can see at a glance where

> When it comes to office supplies, you have two storage needs: a place to put your extra supplies, and places to put the items you use during the day that need to be stored but not hidden away.

everything belongs and the office can keep running smoothly. Put labels on the outside of drawers, on shelves, on clear plastic containers, wherever items are placed when they're not in use.

Before fine-tuning your desktop (see Chapter 5), establish a single place in which to store all of your backup supplies. You can use a closet, an empty dresser, stacking bins, or a rolling storage system—whatever you like that works in your office space. What you want to avoid is stashing small piles of extra supplies in various places around your office and home.

Buying and Storing Office Supplies

When you work at home, it's tempting to store extra supplies in other parts of your abode. Resist the urge to stash items away wherever there's room in your home. Instead of looking for additional places to store supplies, cut down on the amount of supplies you already have. Limiting the number of places you have to look for something will limit the amount of time you spend looking. Also, every time you have to leave your office, you run the risk of getting sidetracked in another part of your home.

If you absolutely have to, build shelves for backup supplies in a designated area of your garage or basement. Reserve this area for items you won't need for a few months. The following ideas will help you store your supplies efficiently so that you'll never hear yourself say, "I didn't know I had that!"

- Store the same type of items together, so that when you look for something, there's only one place to look. Keep all of your pens, pencils, and markers together, all of your filing supplies together, and all backup media storage together. When all related items are stored together, you're never in doubt about where to find something.

- Keep supplies, grouped by type, in clear containers. Label the outsides of the containers and store them next to containers holding related items.

- Post a list near your supplies to help you keep track of what you have and what you need. This list should include everything you need to have on hand.

- Take backup items out of their original packaging to save room. Those clear containers mentioned already are a more efficient use of space.

In the next chapter, we'll take a look at another challenge—how to store the items and papers you use every day so that they are accessible and organized.

QUICK TIP FOR HOME OFFICE PROFESSIONALS

"A place for everything, and everything in its place." Many of us were raised hearing this statement, and it's still valid. It's important to determine, early in your quest for an organized office, where everything will go. If you do this correctly, there will be only one place to look for any particular item, and only one place to store it when it isn't in use.

Clearing Off
Your Desk

Clearing Off
Your Desk

Whether you are setting up a brand new office or organizing an existing one, chances are you have all types of things on your desk. If you're relatively organized already, you might have only some stacks of paperwork, a few pens, some paper clips, some objects you enjoy, and maybe some notes to yourself. If you're not at all organized, you might have old batteries, food, magazines, and who knows what else.

Now is the time to let all of these extraneous items go. Not necessarily into the wastebasket, but into files, into drawers, onto shelves, or onto a surface other than your desk. The only papers on your desk should be the ones you are referring to—the only objects should be ones you use often. That doesn't mean your desk has to look impersonal. It means that your desk should be as functional as possible.

A messy desk is not the sign of a creative mind, nor, as I often hear, is a clean desk the sign of a sick mind. Some people honestly believe that a clear desk will prevent them from being creative, while others realize that a cluttered desk often leads to a cluttered mind.

If you like to keep your desk buried and find that works for you, nothing I say will convince you to change your ways. However, if the clutter starts to interfere with your productivity, make a few modifications along the guidelines that follow.

What belongs on your desk

An ideal way to decide what should and shouldn't be on top of your desk is to ask yourself the following questions:

- Which items do you use every day?
- Which items do you use at least once a week?
- Which items do you use no more than once a month?
- Are there any items—probably decorative—that you never use?

Anything you use daily stays on your desk. Items you use only once a week belong on a secondary surface. Anything you use only once a month should be placed nearby in drawers or on shelves near your desk. Items you seldom use should be stored, and items you never use should be given away or thrown out.

Many people like to personalize their offices with paperweights, photographs, awards, crafts made by their children, and other objects they enjoy. However, you need to strike a balance between a stark office with nothing but the bare necessities and one so filled with personal items there is no room in which to work. Rather than placing knickknacks on top of your desk—your prime work area—move them to another surface. By limiting the items on your desk to those that are work-related and by keeping personal items near, instead of on, your desk, you create a more functional work area. The only items you should keep on your desk are those that you use daily, for example, your personal digital assistant (PDA), a pen and pencil holder and desk lamp. The goal is to leave a space to work and spread out your papers. It's unrealistic to think that everyone can work with a clear desk— they can't—but no matter how comforting it may feel to be surrounded by papers, you still need to make room for the papers that need your attention.

> One of the nice things about a home office is that you have the freedom to include in it whatever you like.

If you can, avoid using a desk blotter. A blotter is useful if you need a smooth area to write on, if your desk has a glare, or if you want to protect the wood on your desk, but it also gives you another place to stash little pieces of paper that will clutter up your work area. If you do need a desk blotter, choose one that does not have a calendar (most do). That way, you won't be tempted to use more than one calendar to record appointments.

> **Don't automatically put your telephone on your desk.**

If your desk is small, you're better off putting your phone (and answering machine if you don't use voice mail) on a surface next to your desk. If you're right-handed, put the phone to your left, and vice versa. That way you can talk on the phone and take notes without getting tangled in the cord. Avoid putting the phone behind you. Constantly swiveling around to answer the phone will only annoy you. The additional surface, either across from or perpendicular to your desk, could be used to hold your computer equipment, files and miscellaneous supplies you use regularly.

If you don't have room for a secondary work surface, start thinking about shelves to hold the items that would otherwise be on your desk. If you keep too many items on your primary work surface, you not only make it more difficult to get down to work, but leave yourself open to accidents, such as knocking a soft drink into your computer keyboard. Get in the habit of maintaining a clear desk as much as possible. If you generate a lot of mess during the day and it doesn't interfere with your productivity, that's fine, but take a few minutes before closing up shop to clear off your desktop again so that the clutter doesn't build up.

QUICK TIP FOR HOME OFFICE PROFESSIONALS

Don't blame yourself for being disorganized. Some of my clients are so ashamed of themselves they ask me to come to their offices secretly so that no one will know they needed help getting things under control. If you're disorganized, don't feel guilty. I know of no formal course in school that teaches organizing skills. How can you know something you've never been taught? Now that you have this book, I hope you'll use it to get organized to a level that suits you. You don't have to be organized to the same degree as someone else. You only have to be organized to a degree that helps you work efficiently and productively.

Organizing your desk drawers

In the next chapter, we'll deal with the stacks of paper that are still on your desk. Before attacking them, however, you'll need to prepare yourself for some filing. This means you need to organize your desk drawers, set up some vertical files, and buy some stacking bins.

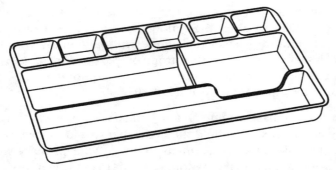

Use trays to organize small office items and keep them from tumbling together in your drawers. (Courtesy of Eldon)

If you look through the drawers in your desk, you may find a junk drawer or two. These are probably filled with things you didn't know where to store, so you threw them into a drawer to deal with them later. Now is the time to sort through these items and separate the useful from the useless. The following steps will take you through this process quickly:

1) Go through one drawer at a time and take out any items you haven't used in the last year. These don't belong in your immediate work area. Try to make the decision right away to throw an item out, give it away, or store it where you can find it when you need it. Because space is probably limited, you may have to be ruthless.

2) Get rid of anything that doesn't work, including dead pens or battery-operated items that have no batteries.

3) Get a box for items you can't bear to part with. Label this box "Hold." If you still haven't used the things in this box after six months, get rid of them.

4) Place all of the remaining items that you use often in a pile.

5) Measure a desk drawer to use as a place to put small things you use every day, such as pens, pencils, correction fluid, tape, scissors, and so on. (A lap drawer is best for this.) Then get dividers to fit this drawer. They will keep your supplies from rolling around every time the drawer is opened. You could also use a silverware tray or an office product designed specifically for this purpose.

6) Consider getting a drawer organizer for your stationery. These store letterhead, second sheets, and envelopes neatly in a drawer without stacking them.

7) If you have a desk file drawer, use it to hold the papers you use often. Keep the papers you are currently working on in files instead of in piles. You'll need this space for files when you start to sort through your papers (see Chapter 8).

   Most desk drawers come with hanging file rods already in them. If your drawer doesn't have a frame in it, you can buy a hanging frame that is easy to assemble, or a freestanding vertical file that fits inside the drawer. You can use either letter- or legal-size hanging folders in your drawer, but I recommend letter-size because they take up less room.

8) Now put the useful items back in your drawers, but this time organized logically. Group like items together, and store the things you use most often in closest reach. Items you use less often can be less accessible, for example, in the back of a drawer or in a bottom drawer. Items you seldom use shouldn't be in your desk, but on shelves elsewhere.

Now that you've organized everything in your desk drawers, you'll never have to waste time searching for lost items. You'll have only one place to look for each item, and you'll be able to see at a glance what you have.

What to do if your desk has no drawers

If you work at a table that has no drawers, you'll need to set up separate holders nearby for the items you use often. If possible, keep these organizers on a secondary surface, not on your desk.

Use any office supply organizer or divided tray to hold your pens, pencils, paper clips, and other small items. Larger organizers have room for computer disks, CDs and other necessities. Office organizers that fit underneath your fax machine or laser printer make an efficient use of surface space.

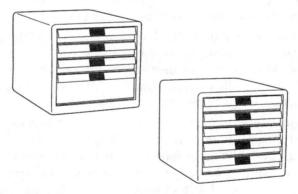

If drawer space is limited, use a letter case to hold stationery and supplies (Courtesy of Iris).

You'll need a vertical file holder or rolling file cart (either stationary or on wheels) in which to place paperwork you are currently working on or files you refer to often. (Current files are discussed in more detail in Chapter 8.)

There are various styles, types, and sizes of freestanding vertical file holders. One type can be used for hanging folders. Made of plastic, wire, wicker or wood, it can be placed on your desk or on a secondary work surface. The benefits of using this type of vertical file holder is that you can use hanging folders for main filing categories and place file folders inside for subcategories.

Organizers that go under your printer or fax machine make efficient use of vertical space. (Courtesy of Eldon)

Another type of vertical file holder holds only file folders. This type has a flat base with equally spaced dividers that stand vertically. Available in metal, plastic or wood, these file holders have a couple of disadvantages: they don't give you the option of using main categories and subcategories when filing your paperwork, and when they get full it's difficult to see the labels on the folders clearly.

A desktop keyboard organizer allows you to push your keyboard out of the way when not in use to give you more work space. (Courtesy of Fellowes)

If you prefer using only file folders, I recommend that you use a tiered vertical file holder. These make it easier to see what is being filed where.

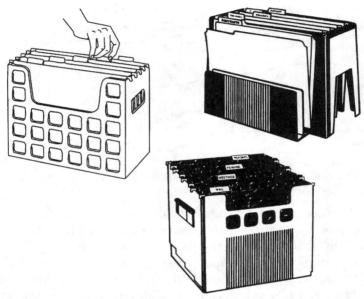

These types of freestanding vertical file holders hold hanging folders and file folders. (Courtesy of Esselte Corporation)

Another option for freestanding vertical files is a rolling file cart. A file cart lets you keep files next to your desk when you're working and away in a closet or corner when you're finished for the day or when you have to clean up your office for visitors. File carts are available in sizes small enough to fit any home office.

QUICK TIP FOR HOME OFFICE PROFESSIONALS

Avoid piles of paper at all costs! Horizontal piles of paper take up valuable surface space, distract you while you're working, and tend to grow higher and higher as you pile unrelated papers on top of one another. It's easier to find a piece of paper if it is standing vertically in a file with related papers than lying horizontally in a pile with unrelated papers. The time it takes to put papers in file folders is minimal compared to the time it takes to sort through stacks of papers over and over to find the ones you need.

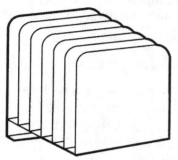

With a tiered vertical file holder, it's easier to see what is filed where. (Courtesy of Globe-Weis)

A rolling file cart provides space for hanging files without taking up desk space. (Courtesy of Organized Living)

The right way to use stacking trays

Traditionally people have kept stacking trays on their desks for "in" and "out" paperwork. As a home office professional, you probably don't really need "in" and "out" trays because in most cases, an administrative assistant isn't going to be processing your papers for you. In fact, it's likely that any "in" and "out" trays on your desk will turn into paperwork graveyards. If you can't bear

Stacking trays, useful for storing stationery or forms, don't belong on your desk. (Courtesy of Eldon)

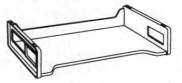

to part with a stacking tray, limit your trays to one, for incoming papers and clear it out each day. Keep the tray on a surface near your desk, not on it. There is a place in your office for additional stacking trays, but it isn't on your desk. Instead, use stacking trays in your supply closet to store your letterhead, stationery, envelopes, and legal pads.

The importance of stacking bins

There are many types of materials you may want to keep close at hand, but not on top of your desk. This material can range from articles to read, to papers that need to be filed, or even packages to mail. Instead of keeping all of this on your desk, use plastic or wire stacking bins. They are larger than stacking trays and can sit on the floor, either under or next to your desk. Stacking bins are inexpensive, easy to use, and small enough to fit any office. They were originally designed to hold vegetables or toys, but they are ideal for organizing papers.

Stacking bins are essential for organizing a home office. (Courtesy of Organized Living)

Label each stacking bin. The following are suggested categories for your stacking bins:

- **To sort.** This bin replaces your "in" box. When you bring papers into your office (for example, the mail), put them in the "to sort" bin until you're ready to process them. You should clear out your "to sort" bin by the end of each day.

- **To read.** This bin is for magazines and newspapers you don't have time to read at the moment but will read later.

- **To do.** This bin is for papers that need action. Before you put any papers in this bin, you should record any action that needs to be taken on your To-Do list (see Chapter 6).

- **To file.** Papers that need to be filed in your file cabinet go here. Papers that should eventually be filed should not be placed on your desk or in your vertical file with papers that need immediate attention.

- **Errands.** This bin is for items you'll need to take with you when you leave the office. These could be sales information, letters to mail, papers to copy, or sales sheets someone is designing for you. Using this bin will help you avoid running out to do errands more often than necessary.

Stacking bins are also useful for large projects—for example, a photographer's stack of photographs, a salesperson's new sales materials, or an editor's book manuscripts. When used in this way, they keep large projects intact and can free up shelf space elsewhere.

Stacking bins provide a temporary place to store papers until you can process them. Even if you don't have time to go through them all every day, by using bins you'll know where everything is. After you've read the rest of this book and you have your paperwork and your time organized, you'll get in the habit of going through your stacking bins at least once a week.

QUICK TIP FOR HOME OFFICE PROFESSIONALS

Always try to move things ahead. It isn't realistic to think you can fully resolve within minutes every piece of paper that comes across your desk. However, you can usually find a way to move things forward if you make an immediate decision and act on it. Even if your decision is to stall, you can file a paper in your vertical files and make a note on your To-Do list to think about it later.

Putting your walls to work

Another way to take some of the pressure off your desk is to think vertically. Shelves, bulletin boards, and wall pockets all keep work-related materials and information nearby without taking up floor or desk space.

Shelves

Adding shelves above or next to your desk is an inexpensive way to gain more storage space. Depending upon how handy you are, installing shelves, whether wooden or metal, is relatively easy.

Bulletin boards

Bulletin boards are excellent for holding memorabilia, for example, a comic strip or a postcard from a friend. Everybody has items like this that, strictly speaking, don't belong in an office but are too enjoyable to throw away. A client of mine keeps "feel good" letters from satisfied clients on her bulletin board in front of her as inspiration.

People who are strongly visually oriented can use a bulletin board to keep track of long-term projects at a glance. For example, Carl, a district sales manager, didn't feel comfortable listing all of his projects on sheets of paper. He was afraid that when he filed his papers, he would forget about his projects. We solved that problem by writing on index cards all of the projects he was working on, then posting the cards on a large bulletin board. Each time Carl looked up, he could see the status of his projects. This system worked so well for him that he ended up adding his sales representatives' projects as well.

Some people would find this approach too stress-inducing. Every time you look up at the board, you realize how much there remains to be done. If this is overwhelming, you may stop looking at the board altogether.

> If a bulletin board would only add to your stress level, don't use it.

If you do use a bulletin board for work-related information, make sure you don't use it for To-Do reminders or important papers that need action. If you use your bulletin board to supplement your To-Do list (see Chapter 6), these tasks will start to fall through the cracks. The longer notes to yourself stay posted on your bulletin board, the more likely it is that you'll just stop seeing them. Your brain will tune them out because they have been there so long they become meaningless. To use a bulletin board effectively, I recommend the following:

- Hang the board on the wall, rather than keeping it propped up against the wall.

- If you use a bulletin board to track projects, divide it vertically into columns and label each column.

- At the end of each month, review the entire board and remove information that is no longer valid.

- When you no longer refer to something on the board, take the item down and throw or file it away. An alternative to a bulletin board is a white board. These boards come in a wide range of sizes, with a special marker that easily wipes off with a cloth. Some come with a preprinted, permanent monthly calendar, a weekly calendar, or blanks in which to fill in tasks to do. These work well for people who plan multiple events or who need to track several projects at the same time.

Another alternative is a magnetic board. You type or write the tasks or projects you want to track on cards (the cards are available in various sizes), then insert the cards into magnetic holders that stick to the board. This option gives you the flexibility of moving tasks forward as you work on a project. Other boards have pockets that hold index cards—all you have to do is move cards from pocket to pocket. Whatever type of board you choose, make sure it is helping you be more productive instead of distracting you or providing a dumping ground for miscellaneous papers.

Wall pockets

Wall pockets, or "hot files," are plastic holders that hang on the wall to hold papers, supplies, or anything else you need to have within reach. Wall pockets can hold about 100 sheets of paper, or four to five file folders. Many people aren't aware that they can use this office-organizing trick to sort and store paperwork they refer to often.

Sally, a representative for a line of clothing, told me during one of my seminars that she had trouble keeping track of her price sheets. She constantly received calls from clients asking her what the latest prices were, and she had to call them back after she'd found her pricing sheets. First I suggested that she use a notebook, but she already had several notebooks for other purposes and didn't have room to store another. That's when I suggested that she use a wall pocket to hold the price sheets. She agreed that this would give her quick access to her papers near the phone without taking up extra space in her home office.

More cheap tricks

Look everywhere for products that might suit your needs. Many items can be used for purposes other than those for which they were intended.

- A horizontal shoe sorter, with spaces for nine pairs of shoes, is a good place to store forms or sales sheets.
- A medium to large sized trash can makes the best office wastebasket because a small one increases the amount of time you spend emptying the trash. Hint: trash can liners make it easier to empty your office trash quickly.
- A silverware tray makes a perfect drawer divider.
- Use a magazine holder, laid on its side, to store envelopes and letterhead vertically.

QUICK TIP FOR HOME OFFICE PROFESSIONALS

Keep the items you use often within reach. Constantly retrieving items you use a lot is as big a time waster as searching for lost items. Every time you leave your desk, you waste time and become distracted. It's important to keep in mind that wasted minutes each day turn into wasted hours each week. Those wasted hours will cost money.

Use a work circle

Before deciding where to put all of your office items, sit at your desk and imagine a circle around yourself. To make the most productive use of both your office equipment and your time, the items you will need on a regular basis should be stored in easy reach within that circle.

Are you always reaching into a cabinet or closet to get your adding machine? Make it more accessible. Are there books or papers you refer to often? Keep them within arm's reach of your desk. Anticipate the reasons you leave your desk, then try to find a way to eliminate the problem.

The following chart will help you gauge how effectively your office is meeting your needs. For one week, keep track of the number of times you leave your desk to search for something you've misplaced or to get something you need.

> Most people are astonished to find out how much time they waste retrieving items that are lost or inconveniently placed.

After you've filled in this chart, you'll see not only how often you're interrupted, but what needs to be corrected within your office.

There are three common types of planning systems: paper-based, handheld and computerized. In the next chapter, you'll learn how to custom-design a paper-based system and in Chapter 7 you'll learn more about other planning options.

Week of _____

Troublesome Item	Item lost	Item out of reach
_____	❑	❑
_____	❑	❑
_____	❑	❑
_____	❑	❑
_____	❑	❑
_____	❑	❑
_____	❑	❑
_____	❑	❑
_____	❑	❑
_____	❑	❑
_____	❑	❑
_____	❑	❑
_____	❑	❑
_____	❑	❑
_____	❑	❑
_____	❑	❑

Creating Your Own Planner

Creating Your
Own Planner

A problem I often see in home offices is lists and little scraps of paper everywhere—taped to the walls, stuck to the phone, pinned to the bulletin board, buried under paperwork. These little pieces of paper are sometimes all over the home—in the kitchen, by an upstairs phone, stuck to the refrigerator. I've seen To-Do lists taped to front doors, phone numbers stuck to mirrors, and reminders surrounding computer monitors.

Ours is an information society. We're bombarded constantly with facts, figures, and ideas. We're also an achievement-oriented society—heavily burdened with obligations, tasks, and deadlines. We have a lot on our minds, and it can be difficult to keep everything straight.

When an important piece of information comes to your attention, your instinct is to grab the first piece of paper available and write down what needs to be done or remembered. The husband of a friend of mine, a cabinet-maker, told me that he writes notes to himself on blocks of wood, since he has more wood in his work area than paper. These pieces of wood do the trick, but they're difficult to file.

What's the solution? Keep a planning notebook in which you record and organize all of this information. A planning notebook allows you to do all of your planning in one place. It is your planning control center—it tells you what you need to do and how to find the information you need to do what needs to be done.

Technology's influence on business can't be overlooked, yet not everyone is computer literate or comfortable with technology. Planning on paper is second nature for many who refuse to switch to a handheld organizer or a computer program.

For those more interested in using a pencil instead of a Palm (PDA) to plan, a planner will keep you on track. If you custom-design your own planner, it will meet your needs exactly. In the next chapter, we'll look at some alternatives, but please read this chapter first so that you understand the full importance of using some sort of personal planning system.

How to design a customized planner

You can easily and inexpensively customize a notebook to fit your needs. To create your own planning notebook, follow these guidelines.

1) **Select a three-ring binder in a size you like.** Your planner can be an inexpensive vinyl binder or an expensive, zippered leather case. Decide if you want a binder that holds 8-1/2" x 11" pages or a smaller size. The size you choose depends in part on how you are going to carry your planner. If you are going to take it with you in a briefcase, you may want the larger size. If you want to keep your planner in your purse or jacket, choose a smaller size.

2) **Add as many subject dividers as you need**. Label the tabs with the headings that follow that are appropriate for you. I recommend that you start with at least the following:

- Current projects
- Monthly calendar
- To do (daily or weekly)

Then add whatever categories from the following list that you would find useful:

- Addresses/phone numbers
- Books
- Client status

- Communication
- Expenses
- Future tasks
- Goals
- Ideas
- Notes
- Personal
- Phone calls
- Reference
- Travel

3) **Add sheets for each section.** Some sections—for example, your To-Do sheets—will require a certain format. You can easily draw up original forms and run off copies for your planner. (Remember to allow space in the margin for the binder ring holes.)

The To-Do section

To-Do sheets are a critical part of any planning notebook, whether you choose a commercially available planner or custom design your own.

QUICK TIP FOR HOME OFFICE PROFESSIONALS

Maintaining a daily or weekly To-Do list is absolutely essential. Studies show that the day you start using a To-Do list you become 25 percent more effective. A To-Do list not only shows what you need to do, but shows what you are—and are not—accomplishing each day. More than a random list of things to remember, your To-Do list helps you organize your time and work more efficiently. If you positively can't stand To-Do lists, use another personal organizing system that will help you keep track of your obligations and accomplishments.

The importance of a To-Do List

When you work at home, it's easy to write a note at one phone, jot down a reminder in your family room, and make another note to yourself in the kitchen, and not bring any of these scraps of paper into your office. Even within your office, you may stick one reminder to your fax machine, another to a file folder, and a third to your desk lamp. If you end up losing both those pieces of paper you lose track of the big picture—all of the things you need to do.

With a To-Do list, you can keep your goals in sight and you know not only what you need to do, but on which day you need to do it. Not using a To-Do list creates a Catch-22 situation— you're too busy to create a list, but you know that using the list

> A To-Do list is the key to getting and staying organized, which is in turn the key to being maximally effective every day.

would keep you from being so busy. Some people who are strongly task-oriented feel it takes less time to perform a task than to write it down. Whatever your rationale, if you don't use a To-Do list, you are failing to take advantage of an essential organizing tool. When you eventually start using a To-Do list, you'll realize why it enables you to work so much more effectively.

A To-Do list helps you set priorities and focus upon important tasks. Part of creating an effective To-Do list is organizing your tasks in order of importance. By writing down all of the jobs that need to be done and then tackling the most important ones first, you guarantee that you will actually make progress every day.

It helps you control your day, instead of letting your day control you. A big time-waster is being in the position of always reacting to situations as they occur instead of creating opportunities to get things done. One of my clients, a retired bank president, told me that he never used to plan his day. He would react to the first crisis that hit his desk and that would set the pace for the rest of his day. When he was in a corporate office, he felt he never had time to plan ahead because he was always "putting out fires." Now that he was in a home office, he had the time to plan ahead, but he had never learned how. He started using a To-Do list and soon got in the habit of listing all of the situations that required his attention and arranging them in order of urgency. Instead of constantly being a fire fighter, he now sets his own goals and accomplishes them.

A To-Do list enables you to be flexible without losing control of your day. A sudden interruption can totally disrupt the direction of your workday. A To-Do list gets you back on track when things aren't going according to plan.

A To-Do list organizes your day. With a To-Do list, you can handle tasks when you feel like handling them. Suppose a good time for you to make phone calls is late in the day. By writing down all of the calls you need to make and running them all at once, you have uninterrupted time to work in the morning.

A To-Do list takes the strain off your memory. If you're constantly trying to remember tasks to do, calls to make, and appointments to keep, you not only live an unnecessarily anxious life but have little time for creative thinking.

Tom, a sales rep, told me he was "cursed" with an excellent memory. He didn't need to write anything down because he could remember everything—his appointments, directions to appointments, calls to make, samples to replenish. I persuaded Tom to use a To-Do list anyway, and he discovered that when he wrote down all of the information he'd been juggling in his mind all day, he was able to think more creatively.

> A To-Do list helps you keep your desk clear.

A To-Do list is an important tool for managing paper. First of all, it replaces all of those scraps of paper mentioned earlier. Second, it helps you organize your work papers. When used correctly, a To-Do list directs you to any piece of paper you need when you need it. If you use a To-Do list in conjunction with filing papers where they belong, or temporarily storing them in a stacking bin, your paperwork will be organized and your desktop will be clear, which helps you focus on one task at a time.

A To-Do list helps prevent oversights. With a To-Do list, you're much less likely to let things slip through the cracks. Better still, you'll record any follow-up action that needs to be taken at a later date, which eliminates the need for all of those reminders stuck to your calendar.

Get in the habit of recording all of the tasks you need to accomplish, both short- and long-term. You'll take a load off your memory, and you'll get more done. Using a To-Do list is a new habit that takes time to acquire. Your level of desire will determine how quickly you assume this new habit. It's definitely a habit worth acquiring.

QUICK TIP FOR HOME OFFICE PROFESSIONALS

Use adhesive-backed notes in moderation. Instead of using them for reminders, use them to write quick notes on papers you send to someone else, or to indicate on your paperwork where documents should be filed. When you need to write yourself a reminder, add it to your To-Do list. Avoid keeping any pads of paper on your desk. Use your planner instead (see page 103). The only exception to keeping a pad on your desk is a spiral notebook for recording phone messages.

Establishing priorities

The most important tip to using your To-Do list effectively is to organize your tasks and calls in their order of importance. After you've written down everything you need to accomplish, use either letters or numbers to rank your tasks and calls from urgent (do today), to important (do soon), to if possible (do eventually). Doing this helps you focus on those activities you need to handle first.

If you number your list, the top-priority task is 1, the next most urgent is 2, and so on. If you letter your tasks, break them into three groups: highest priority, which you identify with the letter **A**; second priority, which you label **B**; and lowest priority, or **C**. You can further refine this by numbering the tasks within each group A1, A2, A3 to indicate their relative level of importance.

Whichever method you choose, concentrate first on your top priority items until they are completed. If your priorities change, renumber (or reletter) your list. If you're having trouble determining which tasks are most important, decide which are the money-making tasks that will enable you to increase your income.

If your list becomes unmanageably long, it will stop being helpful. In addition, the longer you make your list, the more likely you will be to put off working on tasks.

> If your To-Do list—tasks and phone calls—runs longer than 20 entries, evaluate whether certain tasks could be done at a later date.

You will have tasks on your list that are not a high priority, yet may take you only a few minutes to do. It's tempting to do these tasks first. If you know that a certain item will only take a few minutes to do and it's weighing heavily on your mind—do it. For example, if there's an article on your desk that you want to send someone, take a minute to address the envelope and put it with your other letters to mail. The key words are "a few minutes." Avoid small tasks that will eventually take more than half an hour and that were never a high priority.

QUICK TIP FOR HOME OFFICE PROFESSIONALS

Focus on your top-priority tasks every day before working on less urgent tasks. If you are able to accomplish your number one tasks, then you've had a productive day. Strive for a balance between quality and quantity.

Updating your To-Do list

As you complete a task, cross it off your list for that day. One woman I know even went so far as to use a stamp that read "completed" to indicate the tasks she had accomplished. She needed that extra sense of accomplishment to get her through her daily list. Some people get such satisfaction from crossing things off their list that they will do tasks that weren't listed, then write them down so that they can cross them off.

At the end of each day, transfer any item you didn't complete to the next day's list or to a To-Do list for a later date. Then cross these items off your list for that day. It's important to move these tasks forward so that you don't have to flip back to previous lists.

If you find yourself constantly transferring the same To-Do's, use a master project list. Look at it at the beginning of each week, pull tasks from it, and enter these tasks on days when you will be able to do them.

Finding a format that works for you

There are many ways to design a daily To-Do sheet, but all have the day's date, or a place to put the date, at the top. Most have blank lines to the left, in which to record your tasks to do and calls to make, and an hour-by-hour breakdown of the day on the right. Even if you don't have many appointments, the hourly chart can help you block out times to work on certain tasks.

> There's nothing wrong with putting your personal tasks on your To-Do list. However, list them under separate headings, such as "personal," "personal tasks to do," and "personal calls."

Using a weekly To-Do list

Some people don't need a daily To-Do list, but are sufficiently organized with a weekly To-Do list. A weekly To-Do list provides spaces for you to write down what you need to do and the day of the week on which you should do it.

If you use a weekly To-Do list, treat it the same way you would a daily list. Cross off the tasks you accomplish, and at the end of each week transfer any remaining items to a sheet for the week when you will be able to handle them.

Filling in your planner's To-Do section

Once you find an approach that works for you, make sure you have enough daily or weekly To-Do lists for two-three months. This way you can note on the appropriate sheets any tasks to be performed in the days or weeks ahead. Don't keep more than three months' worth of sheets or your planner will get too full. (Tasks to be accomplished more than three months in the future will go in your planner's monthly calendar section.)

To Do		Appointments

To Do		**Appointments**
_____	6:00	
_____	6:30	
_____	7:00	
_____	7:30	
_____	8:00	
_____	8:30	
_____	9:00	
_____	9:30	
_____	10:00	
	10:30	
To Call	11:00	
	11:30	
_____	12:00	
_____	12:30	
_____	1:00	
_____	1:30	
_____	2:00	
_____	2:30	
_____	3:00	
_____	3:30	
	4:00	
Personal	4:30	
	5:00	
_____	5:30	
_____	6:00	
_____	6:30	
_____	7:00	
_____	7:30	
_____	8:00	
_____	8:30	
_____	9:00	
_____	9:30	
_____	10:00	

Try this format for your daily To-Do sheets in your personal planner.
©Lisa Kanarek, HomeOfficeLife.com.

When you open your planner, your To-Do sheet should be on the left, and a blank sheet of paper should be on the right, facing your To-Do sheet. (You can reverse these if you wish—the important thing is to have these two sheets facing each other.) Use the To-Do sheet to itemize your tasks, and use the other sheet to record miscellaneous information for that day (for example, a phone number, directions to an appointment, or your business mileage). At the end of the day, make sure you transfer any useful information from your "miscellaneous" sheet to the correct files in your office.

It's also a good idea to record on the "miscellaneous" sheets any actions you take during the day. One client of mine recently saved himself from having to take a client of his to court by having recorded in his planner all of the activities he performed for his clients. When one of his clients threatened not to pay him, he showed the client that he had maintained written records of everything he had done, and he indicated that he would be ready, if necessary, to produce these records in court. The client paid.

Storing old To-Do lists

When you are finished with a month's worth of To-Do lists— if they're still legible—store them in a binder in case you need to refer to them again. You may find yourself going back to them to track down a mileage figure or a phone number. The amount of time you keep the lists is up to you. Throw them away if you know you'll never refer to them again. Keep in mind, however, my client who avoided going to court.

The monthly calendar section

In this section of your planner, put an entire year's worth of monthly calendars. Make sure the squares on your calendars are big enough to actually write in. Some calendars are so small that only one appointment will fit in each square.

> Your To-Do list is for recording tasks to do, while your monthly calendar is for recording appointments.

Whenever you schedule an appointment, write it down on the correct monthly calendar. You may also want to record the appointment in the hourly section of your To-Do list, if you don't always refer to your monthly calendar. Your monthly calendar will give you an overview of each month, while your daily sheet (if it has a place for appointments) will give you an overview of each day. If you're scheduling an appointment that will take place some time during the next three months—remember, you have three months' worth of To-Do sheets—record the appointment on your monthly calendar. If you're scheduling an appointment further ahead than that, write it on the correct monthly calendar. You want to avoid the possibility of forgetting an appointment because you didn't refer to your monthly calendar.

WEEK OF	
TO DO	DAY

An alternative to a daily To-Do sheet is a weekly To-Do sheet like this one.
©Lisa Kanarek, HomeOfficeLife.com.

The only time you should use a calendar to record tasks is when you don't have To-Do sheets in your daily planner for a future month. For example, if it is May, and someone wants you to call him in September, you would write that on your September calendar, in pencil. When you add the September To-Do sheets to your planner, you would transfer this note to the appropriate day's To-Do sheet, then erase it from the calendar and use the September calendar for appointments only.

Use only one calendar to record appointments. You'll reduce the likelihood of missing or double-booking appointments. You could use a wall calendar for reference only—not to record appointments.

The current projects section

This is a master list of all projects you currently have in progress. List the project, a brief description, and a deadline date. When you complete a project, cross it off your list.

This master list will serve as an overview of everything you need to accomplish. When you take the time to write down all of the projects you're currently working on, they will seem less overwhelming. Each week, look at this list and transfer items that need to be accomplished to the appropriate To-Do list for the week.

The future tasks section

Use this section to list all of the tasks you would like to accomplish in the future but not on any particular day. Writing them down will take them out of your mind and leave you free to think about the tasks at hand. Look at this list periodically, and when you're ready to work on something, take it off the list and put it on a To-Do sheet.

An attendee at one of my seminars showed me a computer printout of his To-Do list. He had 76 tasks on the list. When he didn't get to all of

> A future tasks list is helpful in taking some of the pressure off your immediate To-Do lists.

them each day (which obviously would be impossible), the tasks would automatically transfer to the next day's list. This was all very organized, but not very helpful. I suggested that he create a future task list for his long-term tasks, and that he put on his daily list only the tasks he needed to do immediately. He could then refer to his future task list each week and transfer selected items to his daily To-Do lists. This made his daily lists much more manageable and enabled him to track his top-priority tasks more effectively. You could add a sheet for each month to list tasks you need to accomplish during a particular month if you don't want to list future tasks in pencil on your calendar.

The client status section

Use this section to make notes about conversations you have with various clients. You could use the page facing your daily To-Do list for this purpose. But a separate client status section in your planner enables you to keep a client status sheet for each client.

Some people like to keep client status sheets in their planner, rather than filing them in their client files after every talk. This way they can maintain a running account of their conversations that they can carry with them. Then, when they are waiting for a client in his or her office or in a restaurant, they can prepare themselves by reviewing their discussions.

When you're in your office and speaking with a client, reach for your planner and record the date, time, and the highlights of your conversation on the appropriate client status sheet. By using a client status sheet, you'll eliminate the need for scraps of paper to record notes from a conversation.

When you're out of your office and speaking to a client— either in person or over the phone—the same rule applies. Jot down the important points of your conversation on the appropriate sheet.

The ideas section

Sometimes when you least expect it you get a great idea or a solution to a problem that has been bothering you for weeks.

Usually that idea will come to you at an awkward time—at a restaurant, in a meeting, or while driving your car. Wherever you are, you need to have one place to put those ideas. You may not be able to act on these ideas right away, but at least you'll know where to find them when you need them—in the ideas section of your planner.

The goals section

Some people lack a sense of direction because they don't have well-defined goals. Others are afraid to write down their goals for fear they may actually achieve them. Still others are so busy with day-to-day concerns that they stop even trying to think about where they are headed.

QUICK TIP FOR HOME OFFICE PROFESSIONALS

Take the time to write down your goals, both long- and short-term. For a home office professional, clearly defined goals are essential. No one else is tracking your progress. If you don't know where you're going, how will you know you're on the right track? If you don't pay attention to how much you are doing, how can you be sure you're accomplishing anything?

It's important to write down specific goals you want to accomplish.

Follow these guidelines when setting your goals:

1) **Make your goals realistic.** If you are currently earning $35,000 per year, it may not be reasonable to make $100,000 your goal for next year. Instead, you could set a goal of increasing your income by 25 or 50 percent.

2) **Make your goals specific.** For example, rather than writing down, "Make more money next year," give a specific percentage or dollar amount. This automatically gives you a better way of measuring your performance.

3) **Be flexible about your goals.** Situations change, and a goal that might have seemed appropriate at one time may become less important or less feasible with time. Be willing to change your

goals, if necessary, because clinging to an outmoded goal is counterproductive.

CLIENT STATUS

COMPANY: _____

CONTACT: _____ TITLE: _____

ADDRESS: _____

_____

PHONE NUMBER: _____

DATE	TYPE OF CONTACT	ACTIVITY LOG	ACTION TO BE TAKEN

Using a client status sheet like this one helps you keep track of your conversations with clients.
©Lisa Kanarek, HomeOfficeLife.com.

I have developed a simple goal planner that will help you map out your goals. Take out a blank sheet of paper that will fit into your planner and copy the format of the goal planner below. Then fill in your personal ambitions.

If you realize that a particular goal is going to take longer than you thought, don't drop it from your goal planner altogether. Instead, just move it up a notch so that it's in a more distant category.

Take the time to commit your goals to paper. Look at your goals at least once a week. At the three-month, six-month, and one-year points, see how close you have come to achieving them. You will be surprised at how much you are able to accomplish in a short amount of time.

> Goals are powerful tools that will help you build a successful business.

The tasks you put on your To-Do list each day or each week should be directly related to your goals. If what you do each day doesn't relate to your lifetime goals, then either change your tasks or change your goals.

Goal planner

Lifetime Goals (Add today's date)

In this section, write down everything you would like to accomplish over your entire career. Don't censor yourself. Write down anything that comes to mind. If lifetime goals seem too daunting to plan, start with five-year goals or skip to one-year goals.

One-Year Goals (Add the date in one year)

List here the steps you will need to take to achieve your lifetime goals. For example, if your lifetime goal is to become an expert in your field, your one-year goal may be to read one book a week in that field.

Six-Month Goals (Add the date in six months)

In this section, list goals you could accomplish in six months to help you achieve your lifetime goals.

Three-Month Goals (Add the date in three months)

List here the short-term goals that could help you achieve your lifetime goals.

The address/phone numbers section

There are three options for organizing contact information. You can use a business card file, your daily planning system—whether paper-based, handheld, or on your computer. If you have ever been away from your office and needed a particular phone number but didn't have it and couldn't get it, you'll know how helpful this section can be. Design your own address/phone number sheets, copy as many as you need, and organize them in your planner either alphabetically or by category.

This section works in conjunction with the phone card file that sits on your desk, a business card notebook, an electronic organizer, or a contact management software program. If you pick up an address or phone number during the day, remember to add it to your desk file, daily planner, or computer program.

Another option is to computerize your list by using a contact management software program. With a contact management program, you can print out the names and phone numbers of your clients to take with you while you are out of the office. You have the capability of printing out the names of your clients by zip code, city, state, name, and so on. Don't forget to include your clients' e-mail and website addresses or you can list them under the e-mail/website section.

The books section

It seems that wherever I go or whatever I read, someone recommends a book. Whenever someone gives you the title of a book, turn to the books section of your planner and write it down. Then take your planner with you when you go to the bookstore. A book list works the same way as an office supplies list—it helps you focus on the books you want to buy.

A woman in one of my seminars told me that she used to go to the bookstore every week just to browse, but that she always managed to leave with a new book. When her bookcase started overflowing, she sorted through her books, took out the ones she had never read and knew she wouldn't read, and sold them to a used-book bookstore. Now she keeps a list of books to read and goes into a bookstore with a purpose. She is saving money by not buying books she will never read.

It doesn't really matter how you decide to list your books, so choose a format that works for you. You can list the books you want to read by category (for example, sales, marketing, public relations, or motivation), or you can list them in alphabetical order by title. Listing them alphabetically by author is another possibility, but this can get frustrating because people sometimes remember the title of a book but not the author's name. Whichever approach you decide on, use it consistently.

After you buy a book on your list, put a checkmark next to it. After you've read it, highlight its listing.

The phone call section

Depending upon the company you work for or clients you work with, you may need to keep track of long distance phone calls in order to get reimbursed. You may even get paid for the time you spend on certain calls. Either way, you need a place to record these calls.

A phone sheet makes it easier for you to sort out your phone bill when it arrives. All you need to do is compare your bill with your list and you can quickly tell which calls are personal and which are business-related.

> Design a phone sheet in a format that suits your needs. Include a column for the date, name of the person called, his or her company, and the phone number.

Whenever you make a long distance call or a call to an important client, reach for your planner. Your list will serve as an accurate record of when you called someone, so that when you speak again, you can refer with precision to the previous phone call you made on a certain date. Your phone service probably offers a call-tracking service that would help you save time tracking charges at the end of each month.

The e-mail/website section

Under the address/phone number section, you may have included e-mail and website addresses, but for a quick reference list, include the addresses you use most often in this section.

The expenses section

The requirements for verifying expenses with the IRS leave little room for error. Keep accurate track of your expenses by using an expense sheet. Expense sheets are easy to draw up. Follow these steps:

1) Take a blank sheet of paper that fits into your planner and divide it into five vertical columns that start two inches from the top of the page and run down to the bottom.

2) At the top of the first column, write **Date**.

3) At the top of the second column, write **Type of Expense**.

4) At the top of the third column, write **Amount Spent**.

5) At the top of the fourth column, write **Client**.

6) The last heading should read, **Reimbursable**. Under this heading, you'll write either "yes" or "no."

In addition to expense sheets, you will need to put in this section of your planner a small manila envelope or a plastic zippered pocket with three holes in it to hold receipts during the day. Whenever you incur a business-related expense, enter it on your expense sheet, and then file the receipt in the envelope or pocket. Transfer your receipts to your office files at the end of each day so that they don't build up inside your planning notebook.

Recording your expenses takes a little extra time, but it will save time when you start preparing your tax returns because you'll have a running list of expenses to refer to. Also, in the unfortunate event of an audit, you'll be glad you did it. Using a business accounting software program is another option that is discussed in further detail later in this book.

The communication section

Throughout the day, you may think of things you want to mention to your clients, staff, or spouse. Instead of calling them every time you have something to say, keep a running list of items to discuss.

This section of your planner works best if you keep a separate sheet for each person with whom you are in touch. At the top of each page, write the name of the individual with whom you want to discuss certain points. As you think of other ideas, add them to your list. When you're ready to make the call, refer to your planner.

Using a communication sheet leaves your mind free to concentrate on other tasks. It also guarantees that you won't find yourself saying, "There's something else I want to tell you, but I can't think of it."

The notes section

As a home office professional, you probably attend fewer meetings than your corporate counterparts. Probably the only meetings you attend are with clients. Still, these meetings may generate pages and pages of notes. The next time you're in a meeting, instead of taking notes on legal pads, turn to this section and take notes.

There is an art to taking notes. Your planner can help you make the most of your meeting and can help you make sure you follow up on everything discussed.

1) At the top of a blank piece of paper, write the date and the type of meeting (i.e., staff meeting or client meeting).

2) Draw an "action box" in the right-hand corner of the page. As you take notes during the meeting, record any

action that needs to be taken in the action box. For example, if you need to send information to someone or write a follow-up letter to a client, make a note in the action box.

3) After the meeting, transfer the information from the action box to your To-Do sheets. Then file the rest of your notes in the appropriate file. (This depends on how you have organized your office files. Notes from a client meeting may be filed under the client's name, whereas notes from a staff meeting may be kept in a staff meeting notebook.) If you know that you'll never refer to the meeting notes again, toss the sheets after you have recorded any action you need to take.

The reference section

Use this section as a catchall for information. The listings within your planner's reference section could include the following:

- Pricing information for your products
- Condensed dictionary (these are available in 8 1/2" x 11" pages and smaller)
- Dates to remember (birthdays or special occasions for family members or clients)
- Office supply list for your next trip to the office supply store
- Directions to places you don't go to often, but need to know how to find

The personal section

Use this section to record information about personal projects, hobbies, or activities. You can also insert a sheet for each member of your family.

Getting started

Using a planning notebook and keeping all of the information you receive in one place is a new habit. For the first 24 hours after you design your planner, don't write a single note to yourself on a scrap of paper. Instead, record any information you get or need in your planning notebook in the appropriate section.

Type of Information	Where It Goes
✸ A client's new phone number, street and e-mail address.	✸ In the addresses/phone numbers section or next to your computer to enter in your contact management program.
✸ Request from a client for product samples and/or literature.	✸ On your To-Do list for a particular day.
✸ A phone message with the number of a client who wants you to call back in three months.	✸ In the monthly calendar section, in pencil, on the day you plan to place the call.
✸ Receipt from lunch with a client.	✸ Record lunch on expense sheet in expenses section. File receipt in envelope.
✸ Directions to a new client's office.	✸ On the sheet facing the daily To-Do sheet for that day's appointment. (Or, in reference section, if you have one.)
✸ Note to yourself that you tried to reach someone and left a message.	✸ Next to the entry on your To-Do list, write "mess" to show that you have left a message. On your To-Do list for the next day, write, "should hear from (whoever it is)."

Use the above chart as a reference guide to storing information within your planning notebook.

If any of the previous information was given to you on a slip of paper, toss out the slip after recording the information (with the exception of the lunch receipt). No more little scraps of paper!

Do it your way

Some type of planning system is essential in getting and staying organized. I usually recommend that clients create their own planners if they haven't found one that fits their needs. However, there are other approaches that may work for you. We'll discuss these in the next chapter.

Other Personal Planning Systems

7

Other Personal Planning Systems

There is no one-size-fits-all method for personal organizing. Some people can't be bothered with custom-designing a planning notebook, or need only a simple notebook. Others despise To-Do lists and prefer working with actual papers. Some people don't mind working with To-Do lists, but they become impatient with having to write them out every day. Still others prefer to get organized by writing notes to themselves on index cards.

Whatever your preferences are, there is a personal planning system that will suit your needs. In addition to designing your own planning notebook (see Chapter 6), your options include the following:

- Using a spiral notebook
- Computerized planning
- Electronic handheld organizers
- Using a commercially available planner
- Using tickler files

Any of these systems will provide you with an efficient way to keep track of tasks.

Using a spiral notebook to plan

If you need only a place to record tasks to do and calls to make, a spiral notebook is a good alternative to a planning notebook and loose scraps of paper. A good friend of mine used to write notes to herself on her hand. In that she is a physician and washes her hands many times a day, this method wasn't always successful. Now she uses a small spiral notebook that fits in her coat pocket.

Here is a step-by-step way to set up and use a spiral notebook:

1)   Decide if you want to use a spiral notebook that is bound on the side or one that is bound at the top. Spiral notebooks are available in a wide variety of sizes.

2)   At the top of each page, put every day and date for the next three months. (If you are planning by the week, write "week of . . ." and fill in the dates.) Although you could save paper by entering dates on both the front and back of the pages, you probably will want to enter a date only on the front and leave the back for notes.

3)   Divide each page in half, either horizontally or vertically, and label one section **To-Do** and the other **Calls**. You could also add sections labeled "personal" to record your personal tasks and calls.

4)   In the To-Do section write all of the tasks you need to accomplish, and in the "calls" section write all of the calls you need to make. Organize your tasks and calls according to their level of importance, as was described earlier.

5)   At the end of each day, transfer the items you weren't able to accomplish that day to the next day's list or to a list a few days later. Then cross the items off that day's list and move forward to the next page.

Don't use your spiral notebook to schedule appointments. Instead, use a pocket calendar or desk calendar in conjunction with your spiral notebook. This way you can see all of your obligations at a glance and you'll be less likely to make scheduling errors.

Computerized planning

Personal Information Managers (PIMs) and contact managers are another way to stay organized. PIMs focus more on your time management needs, while contact managers focus more on client contact. If the number of clients you need to track is limited, a PIM should be enough for you. If you want to create extensive mailing lists, track several clients as well as plan ahead, a contact manager would work better for you. Computer planning programs will increase your productivity if you determine what you want a program to do, then find the program with those capabilities. How do you decide if it's worthwhile to purchase a PIM or contact manager? Consider the following factors before investing:

- *Do you prefer planning on paper or on your computer?* You can still use your paper-based system, but have the convenience of a Personal Information Manager. By using pre-formatted sheets, after you enter your schedule, tasks or projects in your computer, print the information, then slip the sheet into your planner. If you manually enter information on your printed sheet, remember to update the information in your computer.

- *Is your handwriting illegible?* Enter tasks, appointments and projects in your computer. You'll no longer have to guess what you've written.

- *Do various tasks ever fall between the cracks?* Keep track of what you need to do and when you need to do it, by entering deadlines in your computer. On the appropriate day, the task will appear on your screen and remind you to handle it. You also can check at a glance the progress of other projects that need your attention.

- *Are your files bulging with correspondence?* Instead of keeping a hard copy of each letter your write, use a contact manager, for example "Act" or "Goldmine" to store it in your computer under the corresponding client's name. When you want to open a person's computer file, all you have to do is type a few letters of his or her name.

Personal digital assistants (PDAs)

PDAs are hand-held, programmable devices that are pen-based or utilize a keyboard. For some people, PDAs have more features than necessary while on the road, while others wouldn't leave home without them. PDAs change constantly. They allow you to send and receive e-mail messages, access client contact information, take photos, synchronize date with your desktop computer and more. Some people prefer PDAs over portable computers because they weigh less, are easy to use, and cost less than a portable.

Small, hand-held PDAs completely eliminate the need for paper in scheduling tasks and appointments. Some people find PDAs awkward to use at first because you look at a screen instead of a piece of paper, but this is actually their great advantage.

PDAs have a variety of functions, including the following:

- To-Do list
- Calendar
- Schedule
- Telephone numbers and addresses
- Calculator
- Memo
- Expense log
- Privacy feature
- Optional computer interface to back up the information you have entered
- Internet access
- Phone
- Digital camera

You can add programs to increase the functions of your PDA. Don't forget to purge outdated contact names throughout the year.

Martin, a home-based sales rep for a long-distance company, made fun of a colleague who used a PDA in the corporate office.

Whenever A.J. heard a new piece of information or was reminded of something he needed to do, he would whip out his PDA. Martin thought this was hilarious, until A.J. pointed out that Martin was always calling him for phone numbers and meeting dates. Martin went out and bought his own PDA, and found that it worked better for him than his old planning notebook because he was more likely to take it with him wherever he went.

The following is a summary of the advantages and disadvantages of using a PDA:

Advantages

- Keeps all of the information you need in one very compact place.
- Extremely portable—fits easily in a purse or briefcase.
- Interfaces with your computer so that you can back up information.
- Ideal for people with poor handwriting.

Disadvantages

- Small screen display may be hard to read.
- Must be careful not to drop it.
- Need to know how to enter information either using letter codes or the stylus to type, unless you enter information on your computer and download it to your PDA, or invest in a small detachable keyboard.
- If you forget to change the battery, you lose everything. (However, the PDA will warn you when the battery is running low and if you backup regularly, you shouldn't have any problem downloading information.)

QUICK TIP FOR HOME OFFICE PROFESSIONALS

Take the time to equip yourself with whatever you need to get organized. This could mean buying anything from a new planner to a new computer. If you don't have the right equipment, you are making your work life unnecessarily difficult. By equipping yourself with the right products, you'll save time and money, and you'll improve the service you give your clients.

Using a commercially available planner

You may decide you want to use one of the predesigned planners available on the market. Planners range in price from $25 to over $200 and come in a wide variety of sizes and formats.

Different planners have various features that you might find useful. Some include plastic pockets for credit cards. Some have To-Do lists that are easy to customize. Some use pages that wrap around each other, eliminating the need to rewrite lists. In addition, some planners are available in software versions.

The *Day Runner* comes with preprinted and blank labels to help you customize your planner. There are also clear pockets that hold credit cards and business cards, as well as a space for your checkbook.

Day Runner refills give you the flexibility to customize your planner. There may be sections you don't need to keep in your planner or ones you want to include. You could add a grid sheet for planning, a contact sheet or a receipt envelope. Determine what you need then find the refills to meet those needs.

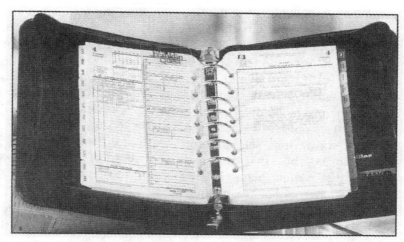

The *Franklin Covey Planner*, available in various sizes and bindings, has a place for your tasks, appointments, and expenses on one page and a place for notes on the facing page.

With a *Day-Timer* planner, each planning page includes an "action list," a phone calls list, an hourly breakdown of day, and a place to record expenses. On the facing page you have room to record notes about projects.

What's important is not the uniqueness of the features in any of these planners, but whether or not they will actually help you. During one of my seminars, a woman told me that she had spent $150 on a planner and that she still wasn't organized. She felt she was a lost cause and would never be able to get organized. After all, if a $150 organizer couldn't organize her, what would? In fact, the problem wasn't that she couldn't get organized, but that she had bought the wrong planner. The sections in her expensive planner

> When buying a predesigned organizer, find one that fits your needs, instead of attempting to adapt to it.

didn't have anything to do with her business, and the way the pages were laid out inside didn't suit the way she liked to record information.

Here are a few tips for selecting the right planner for you:

- Where will you keep this planner—in your briefcase, suit pocket, or purse? Select the appropriate size.

- Is the planner flexible enough for your needs?

- Are there too many sections that don't apply to you? (You can take them out, but why pay for something you don't need?)

- Are the To-Do sheets designed the way you would use them? For instance, are tasks separate from calls?

- Is there enough room to write on the monthly calendar and on the other sheets within each section?

- Does it look professional? If you want to project a certain image, a vinyl-bound planner may appear cheap, whereas a leather one would be more appropriate.

Know exactly why you are buying a planner before you buy it. One of my clients showed me a dozen planners she had bought with the intention of getting organized, but none of them helped. After we sat down and spent some time defining her needs, we were able to choose a commercially available planner that worked for her.

Feel free to tailor a predesigned planner to meet your needs. Experiment with sections you add yourself, and take out (or relabel) any sections that aren't appropriate for you (see Chapter 6). Few calendar companies include a section for personal tasks on their To-Do sheets. If your preprinted planner doesn't have a personal section, add one.

Some people worry that their planner won't look professional by the time they have finished customizing it, but in my view this hardly matters. A polished organizer that doesn't help you is useless. Again, it depends on your type of business. The important thing is to find or design a planner that works for you and then stick with it.

Using tickler files to plan

If you find To-Do lists frustrating, or if you prefer to work with actual papers instead of lists, another personal planning option is a tickler file system, so named because your files are designed to "tickle" you when it is time to accomplish certain tasks. A tickler file system keeps your current papers organized and easily accessible. This is the approach I recommend to people who stuff papers in their planner (a bad idea, because it prevents you from using your planner effectively and your papers can get lost or ruined).

I recommend using a To-Do list over a tickler system or in conjunction with a tickler system because this gives you greater control over the tasks

> Tickler file systems only work if you refer to them daily.

that need your immediate attention. Also, if you choose this approach, your To-Do lists will reflect what papers are in your tickler files. However, I realize not everyone likes To-Do lists, and a tickler file system is better than nothing.

Before I describe them to you, it's only fair that I confess I am not fond of using tickler file systems in place of a To-Do list. A tickler file system is not as precise as a To-Do list. It's easier to ignore, it makes long-term planning difficult, and it increases the time it takes to retrieve papers because you have several places to look for any one document.

There are four basic approaches to tickler files. You can use hanging files, a tickler book, an accordion file, or index cards. How you organize your tickler files depends upon how you like to work.

The next chapter, "Stop Stacking and Start Filing," discusses various types of file folders and filing systems in detail. For now, concentrate on finding a basic organizing system that will work for you.

Tickler File System 1

Here is a step-by-step guide to setting up a tickler file system based on the days of the week.

1) Find a place to store your tickler file folders. Because they are current files, that is, you will be referring to them often, you need to keep them easily accessible. Either store them in your desk file drawer or in a vertical file holder on a surface near your desk (see Chapter 5).

2) Label a hanging folder **Weekly Activity**. Within this folder, place file folders for each day of the week you work. For example, if you usually work Monday through Saturday, label six folders.

3) Into these folders, put the papers you will be working on for the week. In order to do this, you need to determine which projects are most urgent and when you are most likely to handle them.

4) At the beginning of each day, look at that day's folder. Work on those papers all day. If you don't get everything done, move the papers you haven't worked on into another day's folder.

With this system, you keep moving papers forward into the folders for upcoming days of the week until each task is accomplished. For long-term planning, add a folder labeled Future Tasks or Future Projects.

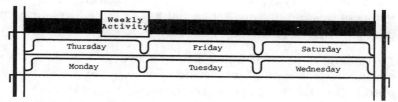

Tickler file system 1 uses a hanging folder with file folders for the days of the week you work. (Feel free to eliminate the Saturday folder.)

Tickler File System 2

Another approach to tickler file folders organizes your papers not by days of the week but according to their relative importance.

1) Find an accessible place to store your tickler file folders.

2) Label a hanging file **This Week**.

3) Insert three file folders. Label these folders **Hot**, **Important**, and **To Do**.

4) File the papers for your current projects in the file folders. Put your most urgent projects in the **Hot** file folder, work that needs to be done soon in the **Important** folder, and tasks that need to be taken care of eventually in the **To Do** folder.

5) Go through the **Hot** file every day, and look through the other files at least once a week. With this system, papers for a project stay in the same file until you take care of the matter or until its status changes.

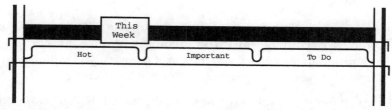

Tickler file system 2 uses a hanging folder with file folders labeled according to your level of urgency.

A variation on this system is to label a hanging file **Hot Projects** (instead of This Week), and to use file folders for each project you need to look at every day.

It's important to go through these files regularly, since tasks change in their level of importance. For example, a task that is only To-Do one week may become urgent the next week. You don't want to ignore projects in the last folder. For long-term planning, add a folder labeled **Future Projects** or **Future Tasks**.

Tickler File System 3

A more involved tickler file system allows you to plan for each day of the month and for upcoming months, just as you would with a planning notebook.

1) Set up a vertical file holder in an accessible place or use a desk file drawer.

2) Label a box-bottom hanging folder **To Do**.

3) Inside the box-bottom folder place file folders for each day of the month. These files will always be used for the current month, so label them only with numbers, not with the name of the month. On April 12, for example, you would look inside the **12** folder.

4) Label another box-bottom folder **Upcoming Months**. Inside, put file folders labeled with the names of all of the months of the year.

5) File papers that need your immediate attention in the **To Do** hanging folder under the appropriate date for the current month.

6) File papers that need your attention in the months ahead in the **Upcoming Months** hanging folder under the appropriate months. Write the exact date that you will need to act on a piece of paper in its top right-hand corner.

7) At the end of each day, move papers ahead. If you didn't get everything done on a particular day, move the papers to another day (or month) when you will be able to handle them.

8) At the end of each month, move papers ahead. When a new month begins, take all papers out of the **Upcoming Months** file for that month and sort them into your daily **To-Do** folders. This will be easier to do if you were good about writing the action date in the upper corner of each paper.

With this system, you must continually rotate papers through your files, adding new projects, moving ahead any To-Do tasks that didn't get done, and cycling in projects that were filed under upcoming months.

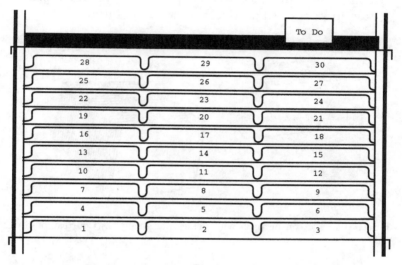

Tickler file system 3 uses a box-bottom file with file folders for all of the days of the month.

Tickler File System 4

This system requires an expanding "accordion" file. There are two types of expanding files—those with dividers and those without. Use the type with dividers.

1) Set up your expanding file in an accessible place.

2) Label the tabs on the dividers from **1** to **31** for the days of the month. Some expanding folders can be bought prelabeled. This folder will always be used for the current month, so it

isn't necessary to add the name of the month. You will not need file folders because you'll simply be putting papers into the pocket behind each tab.

3) File papers that require action under the appropriate day of the month. For example, work you need to do on the twelfth should be filed behind tab **12**.

4) Move your papers forward at the end of each day. If a task hasn't been completed, move it ahead to the next day's compartment or to a day when you will be able to get the job done. A section for **Future Projects** will give you a place to store papers you'll need to refer to in the future.

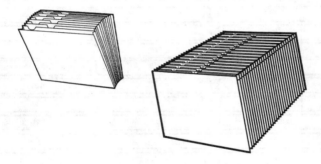

An accordion file can be used with tickler file system 4. (Courtesy of Globe-Weis)

Tickler File System 5

This system is much like the accordion folder system, except that you use a notebook instead of a folder. A tickler notebook comes prelabeled with dividers numbered **1** through **31**. You don't need file folders. Instead, you just file your papers behind the appropriate tabs. An added benefit is that a tickler notebook also includes dividers for the 12 months of the year, enabling you to do your long-term planning alongside your short-term planning.

A tickler file notebook can be used in place of hanging files. (Courtesy of Globe-Weis)

Tickler File System 6

This system keeps you organized by means of index cards. You keep reminders on index cards, but file your actual paperwork elsewhere.

Index cards work well for people who like to write down reminders to themselves on pieces of paper. You can still write notes to yourself, but now you'll have a way to keep them absolutely organized.

1) Get a small file box.

2) Insert cardboard dividers preprinted with the numbers 1 through 31. These will correspond to the days of the current month.

3) Insert cardboard dividers preprinted with all of the months of the year. Place these behind the numbered dividers.

4) Write your To-Do tasks on index cards. Include a card for all current projects that need attention. When you think of something you must do, make a note of it on an index card.

5) At the end of the day, move the cards ahead. If any task hasn't been completed, move its card ahead to the next day or to a day (or month) when you will be able to complete it.

6) At the end of the month, move the next month's cards forward. Reminders for the next month are cycled in as each month is completed.

QUICK TIP FOR HOME OFFICE PROFESSIONALS

Remember to keep your momentum going. It's important to keep up with your filing every week. On your calendar, write "day to file" to remind you to file.

Using your new personal planning system

Studies show that a new habit usually takes 21 days to take hold, so you can expect that it will take you about three weeks to get used to your new personal planning system. Even if you slip up, that's okay. Simply go back to your new and improved system and work to continually maintain it. After 21 days, it should become second nature. This can happen sooner, depending upon your level of desire.

One thing is certain: you won't use your personal planning system if you can't find it. Keep your planner or your tickler files where you can see them.

Jill, an attorney, was disciplined about filling in the To-Do sheets in her planner, but during the day she kept misplacing her planner and failing to check her list. She had no trouble, however, finding her billing notebook. When a client called, she would grab the notebook and record the call so that she could bill the client later. After we designated a certain spot in her office for both her billing notebook and her daily planner, she used her To-Do list more effectively.

> Using a planner, To-Do list, and follow-up system will help you take control of your time and will take you quickly to the papers you need.

Stop Stacking and Start Filing

Stop Stacking and Start Filing

By now you've set up the perfect office. You have a workspace that meets your needs, you've cleaned out your desk, and you have stacking bins to organize your paperwork. However, so far you haven't put this model office to work. It's time to develop a system for handling and storing the papers you are currently working on.

Working styles

Everyone works in a different way and has different organizational needs. The techniques I suggest to one client may not work for another. The first step to knowing which organizational systems will make you more efficient is recognizing your own particular working style.

I've found that most people fall into one of the following five categories:

1) **People who like to keep everything in sight.** For you, out of sight is out of mind. You will lay papers out on your desk or even on the floor to remind you of what needs to be done. You've probably always functioned amidst clutter and have never felt it was a problem. The right organizational systems for you will enable you to put away your papers but still keep them at hand and on your mind. You will find that instead of keeping an entire project in view, it's sufficient to keep only a reminder (your To-Do list) in view.

2) **People who like to stuff everything in drawers.** You are so determined to give your home office an organized look you hide things in drawers or closets without taking the time to process them first. You've got the surfaces under control, which has a calming effect on you, but actually you're generating as much clutter as the person who leaves everything on top of a desk or on the floor. You need organizational systems that will enable you to quickly put things in their proper places. This will keep your surfaces neat and will help keep you from wasting time looking for things.

3) **Perfectionists.** You love details and are concerned about doing things perfectly, no matter how long it takes. You have high standards of excellence. You think you're organized because the items on your desk are perfectly aligned and everything has been typed to perfection. The right organizational systems for you will help you keep your paperwork extremely organized, but with a minimum of obsessing. This will help you focus on the big picture—what you are and are not accomplishing—instead of the insignificant details.

4) **People who jump from task to task.** You have an active mind and have difficulty concentrating on just one thing at a time. You're constantly jumping from project to project without finishing one of them. For example, you make a phone call, then start to write yourself a note about it, but then notice yesterday's mail and start to open it, which reminds you that you'd like a cup of coffee ... and so on. The right organizational systems for you will help you stay focused on one task at a time so that your productivity increases.

5) **People who can't make up their minds.** You hate making decisions because in every situation you see so many possibilities. It's difficult to make decisions because so many approaches have merit. You're afraid that by committing yourself to one course of action you may be closing off another avenue that might be better. You need organizational systems that will help you keep moving papers forward, even if you put off making decisions about them.

Tina and Mitch, husband and wife, were sales reps for a line of costume jewelry. Tina took care of the paperwork (invoices, correspondence, sales reports) and Mitch concentrated on selling (appointments, promotion, following up on leads). Their skills complemented each other beautifully except in their office, where their different approaches created chaos.

Tina was a drawer-stuffer, but Mitch liked to leave everything in front of him. Not only were they getting in each other's way, but between the two of them they had managed to clutter up their entire office.

To get Tina and Mitch out of their mess, we set up some office systems that would work for both of them. Stacking bins appealed to Tina because they provided a place to put things, and they were also okay with Mitch—because he could see at a glance what was where. We brought in a file cart for paperwork, and they rolled it back and forth between the two of them as needed. We labeled absolutely everything so that there would be no question about where items should be stored. We also set up some filing systems to ensure that if one of them filed something, the other would be able to find it. After Tina and Mitch dug themselves out of the mess they had created, they had no trouble staying organized. If they started to slip up, there was already a system in place to get them back on track.

QUICK TIP FOR HOME OFFICE PROFESSIONALS

Don't choose an organizational system you don't like. There's no point trying to implement an approach that doesn't suit your working style. If a particular approach doesn't appeal to you, find an alternative that does. There's always another way to get organized.

Paper, paper everywhere

When you work in a home office, the only limit on the number of piles of paper you create is the space available in the rooms of your home, and possibly a garage.

Melinda, a graphics designer, told the audience at one of my seminars that she had so many stacks of paper she started filling cardboard boxes with pile after pile of papers. When she ran out of boxes, she used her wastebasket. Finally she put the boxes and the wastebasket outside the door of her office, preparing to store her papers in the basement. When she came home from an appointment, she discovered that the housekeeper had thrown everything away, thinking it was trash which, after all, was just what Melinda's papers had looked like. At that moment, Melinda knew she could no longer put off getting organized. People keep stacks of paper spread throughout their office and home for a variety of reasons.

- They haven't made a decision about each piece of paper.

- They want to remind themselves of tasks they need to accomplish.

- They're afraid of filing a piece of paper and never seeing it again.

- They don't have specific places to put their papers.

- They want to keep a document around "just in case."

The solution is to follow the rule "move it forward." Do something to move each piece of paper forward from the minute it comes into your office. You don't have to make final decisions about what action to take, but you do need to decide what you are going to do with the paper involved. First sort, then file your papers until you need them again.

At first it will feel different to do something with each piece of paper instead of just setting it aside. Once you get into this habit, however, you will no longer have stacks of paper in your office.

QUICK TIP FOR HOME OFFICE PROFESSIONALS

To win the paper battle, put your papers to the Paper Test. The more papers you throw out, the fewer you'll have to deal with.

To decide what to toss and what to keep, ask yourself four questions:

- Will I ever refer to this piece of paper again? (If the answer is "no," toss it.)

- Will I be able to replace this paper later if I discover I need it after all? (If the answer is "yes," toss it.)

- Would I jeopardize my job or business if I threw it away? (If the answer is "no," get rid of it.)

- If I need it in the future, will I be able to find it? (If you won't be able to file this paper in a way that will enable you to retrieve it later, and you know you really don't need it, toss it.)

Sorting your papers

The task you are about to embark on will take time, so make sure you block out at least three hours. The following is a step-by-step plan to sorting all of the papers in your office:

1) Have on hand, two sturdy boxes and three stacking bins.

2) Gather all of the work-related papers in your office and throughout your home and put the stacks in one area.

3) Sort these papers into the following five piles. Don't stop to read each piece of paper. At this point, you're only sorting.

- **To do.** These papers need immediate attention. Put them in a stacking bin labeled To Do.

- **To file.** These papers need to be stored in your file cabinet. Put them in your *To File* stacking bin for the time being.

- **To read.** This may include magazines, newspapers, or any other papers you want to read at a later date. These go in your To Read stacking bin.

- **To sort.** These are papers you need to look at more closely after you have set up a current file system (described in this chapter). Put them in the other box.

- **To toss**. Throw out any papers you will never refer to again, including junk mail.

4) Go back to your **To-Do** bin. As you look at each piece of paper, record any action you need to take on the **To-Do** list in your personal planner. (If you chose another personal organizing

system from Chapter 7, use that.) After you've made a note on your To-Do list, these papers should be filed in your current file system, which you are about to create based on the papers in your To-Do bin. Put your To-Do papers in the appropriate bin for now.

Before you actually start filing any of this paperwork, you need to have a basic understanding of filing principles, so let's take a break from office cleaning and move to filing basics.

QUICK TIP FOR HOME OFFICE PROFESSIONALS

Keep your personal and business papers separate. Otherwise, you end up constantly looking through your business files to find the personal files you need. Also, if your spouse handles the personal files, he or she will constantly be in your office looking for them. The ideal approach is to buy a two-drawer file cabinet to use for personal papers. If that's not possible, devote one full drawer of your file cabinet to personal papers only. If you come across stock certificates, bonds, or the title to your car as you're going through your papers, set them aside until you can put them in your safe deposit box. Put information about your credit cards—including the card number and the number to call if your card is lost or stolen—in a personal file labeled *Important Numbers*.

Types of files

There are three types of files: *current*, *reference*, and *historical*. The only similarity among the three is that they are all papers you might like to see again. Keeping them separate makes it easier for you to get your hands on whatever paper you need when you need it.

- **Current files** contain papers that currently need your attention. This could include a letter that needs your response, a report to write, or papers from a project in progress. Current files need to be kept at your fingertips in your desk drawer file, vertical file, file cabinet or rolling file cart mentioned in Chapter 3.

- **Reference files** are those you don't use often, but still need to have accessible. They include any information you may need at a later date, but not on a daily basis. Examples include papers related to clients, past reports you have completed, letters you have sent, and relevant articles from magazines. Reference files belong in your office in a file cabinet (or similar alternative).

- **Historical files** are files you seldom, if ever, refer to, but need to keep for legal reasons. Examples include past tax returns, inactive client files, paid invoices, or any files over three years old. Historical files should be taken out of your file cabinet and stored away safely in a sturdy box labeled with the contents and date.

The P-A-P-E-R system

You have five options when it comes to dealing with paper.

Put it in a stacking bin.

Act on it.

Put it in a file.

Enter it on your To-Do list and file it.

Rid yourself of it (recycle it).

Put it in a stacking bin (or other temporary holding place). Stacking bins are a temporary place to put papers you want to read or file. These papers do not require immediate action. Before you put a piece of paper in your To File bin, write in the upper right-hand corner the name of the reference file where it should go.

Act on it. Acting on a piece of paper means you take action on it at that moment. That could include sending immediate payment to someone or writing a response on someone's note and sending it back (a fast alternative to writing a new letter).

Put it in a file. If you have the time, immediately put papers in the appropriate reference files.

Enter it on your list and file it. For papers that require action soon, make a note of what needs to be done on your To-Do list on the day you are going to take action. Then file the paper in the appropriate current file until you are ready to work on it, or temporarily store it in a nearby stacking bin or tray labeled **To Do**. If you will need the paper as a backup later but don't need it to work on the project, put it in your reference files. Some current papers may not require a note on your To-Do list because they go with information you already have. Put a document like this immediately in the correct current file.

Rid yourself of it. This means either recycle it or trash it.

The saying "handle paper once" has been used for years. It sounds efficient, but it is frequently not possible. Instead, do something with each piece of paper to move it forward. For example, suppose you receive a bill from your printer. You handle it the first time when you open it, but it's not bill-paying time yet. So you file the paper in your "bills to pay" file. When you pay the bills, you'll handle it again. There is absolutely nothing wrong with handling paper this way. What you want to avoid is picking up a piece of paper, wondering what to do with it, then putting it back in a stack on your desk. When this happens, you haven't done anything to move things forward.

Hanging file folders

There are many types of hanging file folders.

- Cardboard, plastic or recycled paper
- Plain or reinforced (to ensure the folder doesn't separate from the metal hanging rod)
- Box-bottom (wide bottom, no sides)
- Hanging box (wide bottom, half sides)
- Two-inch, three-inch, and four-inch widths
- Letter size or legal size
- With or without pockets for storing electronic media

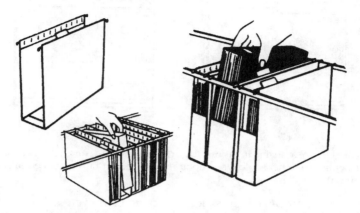

Box-bottom folders (left) have a wide bottom and can accommodate thick files, notebooks, or several file folders. Hanging box files (right) have sides to keep papers from falling out. (Courtesy of Esselte Corporation)

The amount of papers you'll be storing in a hanging folder determines which type to use. Hanging folders are meant to be a guide, not to be taken in and out of your file cabinet or vertical file holder.

File folders

Inside your hanging folders you'll be placing file folders. These are meant to be taken in and out of your file cabinet. There is a large assortment of these, too.

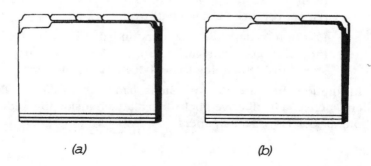

(a)   (b)

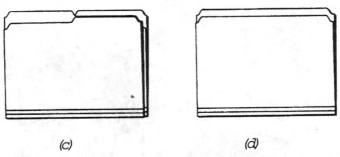

File folders are available in (a) one-fifth, (b) one-third, (c) one-half, or (d) straight cut. Which you choose depends upon the number of tabs you need to be able to see at once.

- Cardboard, pressboard, plastic or recycled.

- Plain files or colored.

- One-fifth, one-third, one-half, or straight cut. The "cut" refers to the number of tabs there are on the upper edge of the folder.

- Plain or scored at the bottom (to allow for expansion).

- Letter or legal size.

- Erasable tabs for relabeling folders.

- With or without fasteners inside to hold papers secure. Fasteners are especially helpful in keeping papers in chronological order.

- With or without sides. A file folder sealed on each end is called a file jacket. File jackets keep papers or electronic media storage from falling out of the folder. Available in plain or expanding versions, they are ideal for holding papers you need to take with you.

- Partition folders use fasteners and divide a file folder into sections, with cardboard dividers. They may be stored inside hanging folders or hung on file rods.

In addition, there are other products made to be used with file folders, such as self-adhesive pockets that attach inside file folders to hold disks, CDs or small papers.

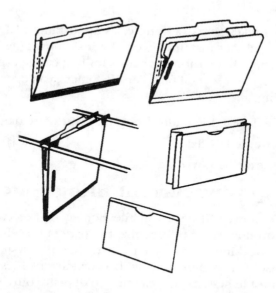

File folders come in a wide variety of types to suit various filing needs.(Courtesy of Esselte Corporation)

Labeling hanging folders

Take the time to carefully label your hanging folders. This will save you time later when you're looking through your files. For hanging folders, you can use either of the following:

- Plastic tabs (clear or colored), with white inserts you write on.
- Tabs you write directly on, then attach to your folders.

The big question with hanging folders is whether to put the plastic tab with the label on the front or the back of the folder. This is entirely a matter of preference. It doesn't matter which approach you choose, but I do recommend that you be consistent. That way you won't put papers in the wrong folders because you pushed a folder back when you should have pulled it forward.

Labeling file folders

Although it takes an extra minute, it's important to label your file folders as well because they won't be inside hanging folders when you're using them. Labeling makes refiling easier, especially after you've taken out several files. For file folders, you can use any of the following:

- Self-adhesive file folder labels that you write on
- Electronic labeler
- Your own handwriting

Setting up your current filing system

In a desk drawer file, vertical file holder, or file cart (see Chapter 5), you now want to organize the papers on which you are currently working. If you set up a tickler file system (see Chapter 7), use it in conjunction with your current files. If you have a hanging file system, use hanging folders. If you're using a vertical file holder that accommodates only file folders, skip the following steps for hanging folders.

1) Start by labeling a hanging folder **Action**.

2) Inside this hanging folder, put two file folders labeled **To Do** and **Pending**. (You may prefer **Follow-Up** instead of **Pending**.) If you write letters to prospective clients and are waiting to hear from them, you could add another folder labeled **Prospects**.

3) Label another hanging folder **Bills**. Stagger the plastic tabs on your hanging folders so that you can read them.

4) Inside this hanging folder, place a file folder labeled **Bills to Pay**. If you pay bills twice a month, instead of using Bills to Pay, use two folders labeled **1** and **15.** If you charge any business purchases, add another file folder labeled **Charges**. Stagger the tabs on the file folders (left, middle, right) so that you can read them. (Consider online bill paying as a way to save time handling paper each month.)

5) Label another hanging folder **Projects**. Inside put a separate file folder for each of your current projects.

6) Add any other categories you may need, based on the papers in your To-Do stack. For example, you might need a hanging folder labeled **Orders**, with file folders labeled **Orders to Place** and **Pending Orders**. Or you might need a hanging folder labeled **Letters**, with file folders labeled **Letters to Write** and **Waiting for Response**. If you have staff working for you, you might create a **Staff** hanging folder and put in it a file folder for each staff member.

To be extra organized, use a different color for each group of hanging and file folders. For example, all of your file folders under **Bills to Pay** could be green.

> Avoid labeling any files Miscellaneous. That's an open invitation to keep papers you will probably never refer to again, or at least won't be able to find.

Using your current file system

Now you're ready to file your To-Do stack. This is the point at which some of you will learn that *out of sight does not have to mean out of mind*.

Before you file anything in your current files, remember to make a note of any action necessary on your To-Do list. This will wean you away from the habit of keeping papers on your desk in order to remind you to take care of them. Next to the notation on your list, you could put the name of the file in which you place the related papers. This way your To-Do list will take you directly to the correct papers. If you want to keep papers out but organized, use a stacking bin labeled **To Do**. Before you put a piece of paper in your To-Do bin, make a note on your To-Do list of any action you need to take.

Use the hanging folders and/or file folders you just set up to file your To-Do papers. When you come across papers that don't fit into an existing category, set them aside until you're finished filing the rest. Then go back and decide if you should start a new folder for these papers in your current files, if they could possibly go in your reference files, or if you can toss them.

1) In the **To Do** folder, put the papers that need immediate action.

2) The **Pending** (or **Follow-Up**) file folder is for papers that need some type of response from someone else or some type of action from you at a later date. For example, if you sent a letter to a client and are waiting to hear back from that person, keep the letter in your **Pending** file. If you attend seminars often, you could add a file folder labeled **Seminars** and keep related information about upcoming seminars that you will be attending.

3) File your bills under either **Bills** or **1** and **15**, depending on how many folders you created for bills. Put charge receipts in your **Charges** folder. (Later you can compare them against your bill.)

4) Group any paperwork about current projects in the **Projects** hanging folder in the appropriate files. Each project should have its own folder.

> **Exception #1** is any project that has generated only one or two pieces of paper. Projects with little paperwork can be grouped together in a file folder labeled **Ongoing Projects**.

> **Exception #2** is any project that has generated a lot of paper. If a file folder is more than an inch thick, it deserves its own hanging folder, labeled with the name of the project, and filled with separate file folders corresponding to various aspects of the project.

After you have sorted your **To-Do** pile, go back to your **To Sort** pile and decide what to do with those papers. If any of them fall into the To-Do category, you now know what to do with them.

When you are finished, there shouldn't be any stacks of paper left on your desk. All of your papers should have been stored in your current files, placed in stacking bins, filed in your reference files or thrown away. Here are some examples of how to process papers by using your To-Do list.

Piece of Paper	To-Do List
✴ A letter from a client requesting information.	✴ Write down or enter in your contact management program (see chapter 13), "Send information to XYZ," then file the paper in the client's file or toss it.
✴ A brochure describing a seminar you want to attend.	✴ Write down, "Send registration form and check for seminar." Place the sheet in your To-Do bin or file and enter the date in your calendar.
✴ A brochure describing a conference you might want to attend.	✴ On the To-Do sheet for the appropriate day, make a note of the deadline for registration. Then put the brochure in your To-Do bin or folder.
✴ Notes from a recent conversation with a client.	✴ Transfer any items from your action box to your To-Do list, then put the notes in your To File stacking bin or toss the notes if you've entered the information in a contact management program.
✴ Your phone bill.	✴ Check the payment due date. Write down "pay phone bill" or "pay bills" a week ahead of that date to avoid late charges. Contact the companies that bill you regularly to try to synchronize the date all bills are due.

QUICK TIP FOR HOME OFFICE PROFESSIONALS

Never store papers flat. Papers are easier to find when they are stored vertically in files, rather than horizontally in piles. The only time your papers should be stored horizontally is when you place them in stacking bins, and this is only on a temporary basis. Eventually the papers in the bins will be stored vertically or thrown away (recycled).

Clearing out your current files

Once no further action is required, papers should go in reference files (see Chapter 9) or be tossed. Go through your current files often (more than

> Current files are for
> papers that need action.

once a year) to get rid of papers that don't belong there. When a particular file gets too full, see if you can toss any outdated papers inside. You need to keep papers continuously flowing through your current files. If you don't, your current files will start to fill up with reference files, which will make it more difficult to find the papers you need right away. It also makes it more difficult to focus on the tasks that need immediate attention.

Getting rid of stacks of paper in your office is the first phase of paper control. In the next chapter, you'll learn how to make your reference files manageable.

Home Office
Filing Systems

Home Office Filing Systems

No matter what size your home office is, you will need to have some type of filing system that goes beyond the current file system described in Chapter 8. Whether you need several file cabinets or just a milk crate to hold your files, the key is to be able to quickly find the papers you need.

I've seen file cabinets used for all sorts of things. Some people use them for all three types of files: current, reference, and historical. Some people use them to store office supplies. Many people, when they run out of room, go out and buy more file cabinets, file crates, or file carts. However, before you invest in more file cabinets, why not clean out the files you already have?

Now that you've taken all of the unnecessary items out of your office and removed all of the unnecessary things from your desktop, it's time to purge your files.

Two types of reference files: Current and Older

In Chapter 8, you were given procedures for setting up current files for papers you are currently working on. Now you will turn your attention to papers that you may want to look at again someday, but that you don't need to have at your fingertips.

You already know from Chapter 8 that these remaining files will fall into two categories: reference files (keep accessible) and historical files (store where you'll be able to find them if necessary). Most home office professionals find it useful to subdivide their reference files into two subcategories—current reference and older reference.

Current reference files are different from *current files* because they are used often, but not on a daily basis. Examples of current reference files include the following:

- Backup documents for current projects
- Client files
- Sales materials

Older reference files contain papers from past projects or events. You may refer to these files once or twice a month. Examples of older reference files include the following:

- Articles from magazines
- Competitive information
- Notes from a seminar you attended
- Past client information

As you sort the remaining papers in your office, you will need to start thinking in terms of four file categories:

1) Current
2) Current reference
3) Older reference
4) Historical

Once you get in the habit of thinking this way, all of your filing decisions become much easier.

Purging your files

You may have stacked your paperwork in your **To File** stacking bin, or you may have files already in file cabinets. If they're in your cabinets, go through them one drawer at a time.

If you're a pack rat, you may be faced with an overwhelming number of files. Going through your files and keeping only the ones you need may seem to be an impossible task. Don't be surprised if your office looks

> Be prepared for unsolicited advice from family members and friends while you are elbow deep in files.

worse during this sorting process than it did when you started. Keep in mind that this disaster is only temporary, and that when you're finished your office will look much better than it did originally.

Throughout the sorting process, don't stop to read every paper. Just sort. It's important to make a quick decision about each file. Here is a step-by-step guide to purging your files:

1) *Sort all your paperwork into four piles:* **Current Reference**, **Older Reference**, **Historical**, and **To Sort**. Your current files and personal papers should all have been taken care of (see Chapter 8). Have a trash can nearby for papers to toss (recycle).

2) *First deal with your historical files.* Put them in sturdy boxes with a lid. Then label them with the date and the contents. Store these files in a closet, preferably in your office, otherwise on pallets in your garage, basement, or attic. If storage space is limited, you could take them to be microfilmed or store them off-site in a storage unit. Before you spend the money on these alternatives, make sure the information you are keeping is worth saving. The point is to keep your historical files out of the mainstream of your home office.

3) *Now turn your attention to your pile of current reference files.* For the next level of organizing, start grouping similar current reference files together. For example, your client files should all be together.

4) *Place your current reference files in the top drawer of your file cabinet, or the part of the cabinet that is most accessible.* Later on you will learn more about various filing systems, but

for now all you need to do is put your current reference files in your cabinet.

5) *Organize your older reference files into groups*, as you did with your current reference files.

6) *Put your older reference files in the bottom drawer of your file cabinet, or the part of the cabinet that is least accessible.*

7) *Before you go any further, go through each file and take out papers you no longer need.* Remember the Paper Test on page 145. Avoid the tendency to jump from drawer to drawer. Start with one drawer and work on it until you're finished. As you go through each drawer, you will find files that belong elsewhere. Either keep them in a stack on the floor until you get to them, or go ahead and place them in the correct drawers.

8) By now you should have taken care of all of your historical, current reference, and older reference files, as well as any current files or personal papers that might have sneaked into this process. Look at your **To Sort** pile last and decide which category is appropriate for each file. You may be surprised to find, as you look through this pile, that most of the items will be strong candidates for the trash.

QUICK TIP FOR HOME OFFICE PROFESSIONALS

Give your files names that will immediately come to mind when you need a piece of paper. Use word association. There is no general guide to naming files—this is a very individual matter. What works for you may not work for another person. The only filing system that will work for you is one that is customized to meet your needs. In a home office, you'll probably be the only one using the files, so it doesn't matter if the names mean nothing to anyone else. However, if anyone else will be using your files, explain your system to him or her.

Filing 101

Before you set up filing systems within your file cabinet, review the following filing basics:

1) Make sure your file cabinet has a frame for hanging folders inside. Always use hanging folders in your file cabinet, and always use file folders inside the hanging folders. Hanging folders are not designed to be taken in and out of your cabinet regularly.

   Some people just stuff their file folders in their file cabinet drawer, maybe with some cardboard dividers between them. This is a bad idea. It takes longer to find the file folder you need because it's difficult to read the labels on the tabs, the folders often slip down because they have little support, and you have a tendency to ruin folders and make the labels illegible because you're constantly pushing and pulling on them. When you use hanging folders, you pull on the hanging folder, not on the file folder itself

2) A topic doesn't really deserve its own file folder until you have accumulated about eight pieces of paper for it. Until then, group related topics together in one file folder. For example, suppose several people wrote to you inquiring about your services, and you answered each of them with a simple letter. Staple your responses to the original letters and file all of this correspondence together. If one person turns out to be serious about what you have to offer and you end up exchanging several letters, it's time to label a new file folder with the name of that individual. Another option is to keep letters stores electronically (see Chapter 13).

3) Use more than one file folder within each hanging folder. You don't need a separate hanging folder for each project or client until the file folder starts getting too full. Too many hanging folders means too many places to look for one piece of paper. They also take up more space in your file cabinet.

4) Keep your folders up to half an inch thick (about fifty sheets). When they get thicker than that, divide the file folder into subcategories. For example, suppose you have a hanging folder labeled **Projects**, and inside there is a file folder labeled Wilson Project that is getting too big. Divide the Wilson folder into file folders for various aspects of the project. Then label a hanging folder Wilson Project and put the file folders in it.

5) Create an index that lists all of your hanging and file folders. This reduces the chance of your duplicating files. Also, when you need to find a piece of paper, the index will help you go to the right file. The best place to keep your index is in a file folder labeled **Index**, inside a hanging folder with the same name and kept at the front of your file cabinet.

A sample portion of your index might look like this.

> FORMS (HANGING FOLDER)
>
> Client contact forms (file folder)
>
> Order forms
>
> Project planner forms

6) Before you file a piece of paper, write in the top right-hand corner the name of the file where it belongs. Another option is to highlight a key word that corresponds to an existing file. If you need to create a file, write the new file name in the corner of the paper or attach a sticky note with the new file name written on it. (There are preprinted sticky notes available that have the word "file" on them.)

When you put the names of the correct files on your papers, the next time you take them out of your file cabinet, you'll know exactly where they belong. You'll also save yourself the headache of creating new files unnecessarily because you weren't certain if an appropriate file already existed.

7) After putting the name of the file in the top right-hand corner, put a purge date at the top as well. This makes it easier to throw away papers you no longer need. Every time you take out a file, throw away any outdated papers. In addition, go through your file cabinet at least every six months and get rid of papers you are no longer using.

8) Label the outside of each file drawer. That way you'll save time opening and closing drawers, looking for files.

9) Stagger the tabs. Do this on the file folders within each hanging folder and on the hanging folders so that you can easily see each one.

10) If you're hard on file folders, for example, if you take the same one out a lot, consider buying file folders made of plastic that can withstand the wear and tear.

11) Avoid filing papers with paper clips attached. These bulk up your files. Even worse, they often catch on other papers and make it difficult to find the papers you need.

Letter or legal size?

I am often asked which size folder is better, letter size or legal size. Unless you are in the legal profession, most of your documents will probably be letter size, making legal-size folders unnecessary. Letter-size folders, because they are smaller, also make a more efficient use of space.

> If you inherited a legal-size file cabinet, you don't have to use legal-size folders. Instead, buy a letter-size file frame, put it in the drawers, and hang letter-size hanging folders on it.

Hanging folders vs. accordion folders

I prefer to use hanging and file folders, but realize that some people are partial to accordion folders. Your choice of folders depends upon the type of information you're filing and the amount of file space you have, or if you need to take files with you.

Finding the right filing system for you

There are three basic types of filing systems you can use with hanging and file folders. You have the option of filing your papers according to one of the following systems:

- Alphabetically
- By category
- Numerically

The papers you are filing can be broken down into three categories:

    1) By type (bills, letters, reports)

    2) By name (corporation or individual)

    3) By geographic location (city, state)

The key to filing is to make the system fit your needs and to make the retrieval of papers easy. Using color with any filing system makes it possible to file and retrieve papers more easily and more quickly.

Alphabetical order—what comes first?

Whichever filing system you choose, you need to be familiar with the correct way to put files in alphabetical order. The following are some all-purpose rules for filing alphabetically:

1) File nothing before something. For example:

    Jones, William

    Jones, William A.

    Jones, William C.

2) Spell out numbers to file them. For example, the numbers 1, 2, 3, 23, and 71 would be filed as follows:

    one

    seventy-one

    three

    twenty-three

    two

3) Put last names before first names. For example:

    Brown, J. (not J. Brown)

    White, L. (not L. White)

4) Completely spell out company names and then file them by the entire name. For example, use Madison Franklin Enterprises, not Enterprises, Madison Franklin, or Franklin Enterprises, Madison.

5) Disregard articles (a, the) when filing. For example, *The Book of Lists* should be filed under B.

Alphabetical filing systems

The alphabetical filing system is ideal for the following types of files:

- Clients
- Company information
- Research information

This is the most basic filing system, and it is often used in home offices. It works well when it is applied to the right types of papers and when one main subject will be placed in a file drawer.

John, a financial planner, filed all of his papers alphabetically. This worked well for filing his client information, but fell apart with other topics. As his files began to grow, related information ended up being stored in different drawers of his file cabinet, and he discovered he was spending too much time searching for the files he needed. John's files looked something like this.

Bane, William [client]

Bills to pay [current]

Boy Scouts [information about his son's troop]

Brian [his son]

Brown, John [another client]

Budget [current]

Budget [from three years ago]

Part of John's problem was that he was stuffing file folders into his file cabinet without using hanging folders. This contributed to the lack of organization in his office and the amount of time he was wasting looking for files. In addition, there were several other things wrong with his system.

- Current files were mixed up with reference files.
- Personal and business papers were stored together.
- Client files were mixed with other files.

The first thing John had to do was set up a separate location for his current files. Then he had to sort his papers as we just discussed, putting the historical files into storage, placing the personal papers in a separate drawer, and separating current reference files from older reference files. After investing in hanging file folders, John was ready to pick a better way to refile his paperwork.

Alphabetical Filing System 1

The following is a basic approach to alphabetical filing:

1) Label tabs on hanging folders with each letter of the alphabet. You'll probably want to stagger the tabs so that they are easier to read. Box-bottom hanging folders are useful for thick files.

2) Within the **A** hanging folder, place file folders for subjects that begin with the letter "A". Limit the file folders to four or five per hanging folder (depending upon the thickness of each file folder).

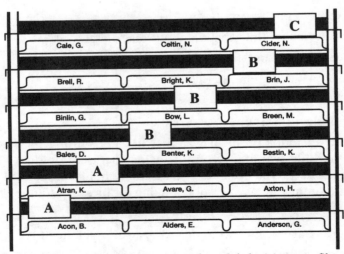

Alphabetical Filing System 1: a basic approach to alphabetizing your files.

3) If you have more file folders to file under **A**, start another hanging folder for them. You can add another **A** tab, or skip adding any more tabs until you get to **B**.

Alphabetical Filing System 2

This system adds a "catchall" file at the beginning of the files for each letter. Use these extra folders to hold papers that do not have their own files. When you have enough papers that are related to one another, start a file folder for these.

1) Set up your files as in Alphabetical Filing System 1.

2) Label an extra hanging folder for each letter of the alphabet.

3) Inside these hanging folders, add file folders labeled with the corresponding letters of the alphabet.

4) Place these extra hanging folders at the beginning of the files for each letter of the alphabet.

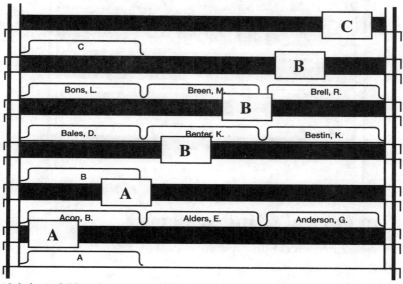

Alphabetical Filing System 2 includes catchall hanging folders for each letter.

Alphabetical Filing System 3

I recommend that you avoid filing all types of papers together. However, old habits are sometimes difficult to break, and you may find it easier to group all of your paperwork together, no matter what the subject, and file your papers strictly alphabetically. If that's the case, do the following:

1) Label a catchall hanging folder for each letter of the alphabet as in Alphabetical Filing System 2. Use this folder for papers that don't have their own files.

2) Behind these hanging folders, file your papers alphabetically. Group your papers together as much as possible, and label each hanging folder with a main category (for example, Accounts, Advertising, Articles). Inside, file subcategories in labeled files. Box-bottom hanging folders may be helpful.

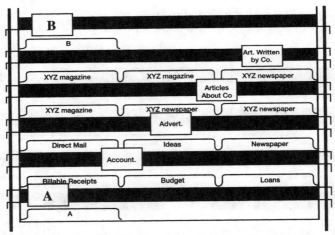

Alphabetical Filing System 3 groups papers alphabetically by topic.

Categorical filing systems

The categorical filing system is ideal for the following types of files:

- Articles on specific topics
- Associations
- Forms
- Projects

- Receipts
- Sales sheets

With a *categorical filing system*, you group similar information. This system uses the principle of a main category and subcategories, with the hanging folder used for the main category and file folders used for the subcategories. Filing by category has several advantages.

1) Related information is kept together.

2) You have fewer places to look for each piece of paper.

3) Files are in bite-size pieces.

4) You don't need to cross-reference your files because similar papers are already grouped together.

The following outline is an example of a categorical filing system:

ADVERTISING

Direct Mail

Newspaper

Radio

ASSOCIATION (GIVE NAME)

Correspondence

Newsletters

FORMS

Fax Cover Sheets

Invoices

Order Forms

Prospect Sheets

Standard Contract

MARKETING

Clubs for Speeches

Cold Calling

Direct Mail

How to Set Up a Categorical Filing System

The basic approach to categorical filing is as follows:

1) Group your file folders together by main category.

2) Label a hanging folder with the name of each main category and place the file folders inside in alphabetical order.

3) Place the hanging folders in your file drawer either by category in order of importance or alphabetically. The alphabetical approach is simplest, but it may be problematic for you if you'll constantly be reaching into the back of your file drawer for a folder that's filed under V.

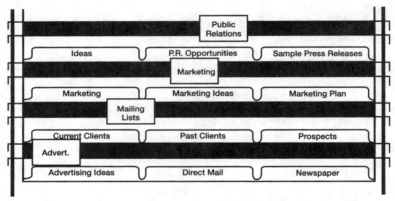

With a Categorical Filing System, you file papers alphabetically within categories.

You could use a different colored hanging file tab for each overall category. This way, when you open your file drawer you'll easily see the separation of files by category.

Numerical filing systems

The *numerical filing system* employs numbers instead of letters or words. This filing system is ideal for the following types of files:

- Confidential files
- Invoices
- Temporary files

The advantages of filing numerically are the following:

1) **Privacy**. If your office is also used as a guest room, your guests won't easily be able to tell what is inside each file folder. Unless you're familiar with the system, it would take awhile to find a particular folder.

2) **Speed.** When you need to find a piece of paper, you look at the numerical index and it will take you right to it. Numbers are easier to locate than names.

3) **Flexibility.** If you throw away the contents of a folder, you can still use the folder for a new subject. There's no need to relabel a file folder. All you have to do is update your index.

The following outline is an example of a simple numerical filing system:

1. ADVERTISING

A. Direct Mail

B. Newspaper

C. Radio

2. MARKETING

A. Marketing ideas

B. Marketing plan

This is the least complicated numerical system you could use. Numbers don't work for everyone, but they are an option to consider.

How to Set Up a Numerical Filing System

The following is a basic approach to numerical filing:

1) Label each hanging folder with a consecutive number.

2) Create a computerized index that is easy to update.

3) Group your file folders by category or subject.

4) Label the file folders with the number of a hanging folder and place them inside the appropriate hanging folders.

5) After staggering the tabs on the file folders, add a letter to each one (1A, 1B, 1C).

6) Enter an overall description of the contents of each folder on your index.

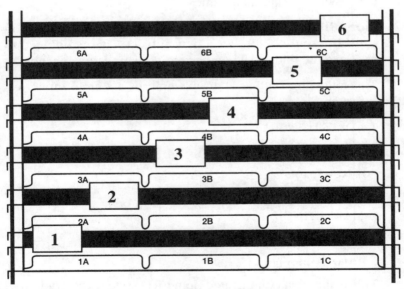

With a Numerical Filing System, each folder is given a number instead of a letter or word.

Color coding your files

> Color-coding may be used with any filing system. With the color-coding method, colors are used to visually separate letters, categories, or numbers.

You can use colored hanging folders, colored file folders, and/or colored tabs on the hanging folders, depending upon how involved you want to get. Within an alphabetically arranged file drawer, for example, the A's could be red, the B's yellow, and the C's blue.

With a categorical filing system, each category could be a different color. With a numerical system, numbers 1 through 25 could be one color, or the files that relate to one another could be one color.

Some home office professionals use different colored folders for different file drawers. Everything in the top drawer, for example, goes in a red folder. This makes refiling easier. To save money, you could buy colored hanging file tabs only and use file folders inside, or match a colored self-adhesive file label with a hanging folder tab.

Some people feel it's easier to get organized when they use colors. Judy, the office manager of a four-person home office, had struggled with getting organized for years. She found the standard filing methods too rigid. For her, we devised a filing system and a daily planning system based on colors. The papers that needed her immediate attention were placed in red folders, and those that had to do with finances were in green. She had to keep track of the schedules of two bosses, and so she gave each one a color. On her daily To-Do list, she highlighted the tasks in colors that corresponded to the appropriate folders. Less visually oriented people sometimes made remarks about Judy's "rainbow office," but the fact was, this system worked for her where others hadn't.

Filing in binders

Some people prefer to file their papers in notebooks or binders instead of file folders. One of my clients, who worked in finance, had over the years built up a bookcase filled with binders that were clearly labeled and in which he could find anything he needed.

If you have more shelf space than file space, try using three-ring binders to free up your file cabinet. This way you can keep papers such as warranty information on your shelf instead of having them take up space in your file drawers.

Binders will work well if you do the following:

- Clearly label the outside of each binder.
- Store related information within one binder.
- Use dividers within each binder to separate the various sections.
- Keep a three-hole punch accessible to make it easy to quickly punch holes in the papers and put them in binders. If you don't want to punch holes in your papers, use clear plastic sheets that slip easily into a binder.

If you prefer using binders but have more file space than shelf space, there is a way around this problem. Buy plastic binders that hang on file rods.

Store notebooks in file cabinets by using hanging binders. (Courtesy of Avery)

Getting started

The most difficult part of implementing a new filing system is getting started. Go back to your file cabinet and start thinking about the best filing system for you. Make copies of the chart on page 175 and use it to plan your own filing system.

When you are completely overhauling your files, it's helpful to get your new system down on paper before you start labeling files. You'll have fewer surprises, and you'll spend less time moving tabs around and working in folders you forgot about.

File planning chart

Use this chart to write down the contents of your files before you go through the process of labeling your folders.

FILE PLANNING CHART

Use this chart to write down the contents of your files before you go through the process of labeling your folders.

Main Category	Subcategories

QUICK TIP FOR HOME OFFICE PROFESSIONALS

The Three-Minute Paper Test. If you can't retrieve any piece of paper you need within three minutes, your filing system isn't working. Taking more than three minutes to find a document is like taking the local train through all stops when you could have taken an express. As a home office professional, you don't have that kind of time to waste.

Troubleshooting your files

In my years of helping clients organize their offices, I've discovered a few problems associated with filing. The following are the most common, with the solutions I've devised for them:

Problem: File folders are sticking out of the top of hanging folders.

Solution: Limit yourself to four or five file folders within a hanging folder (based upon the thickness of each folder). When a hanging folder gets to be one and a half to two inches thick, start a new one. Another option is to use a box-bottom hanging folder.

Problem: A file folder that is too full.

Solution: Divide the papers into separate file folders, then put them in one hanging folder labeled with a name that describes the overall category of the file folders.

Problem: Can't see the tabs on hanging folders.

Solution: Use file folders that are cut lower. Also, make sure your papers are completely in the folder before you put it away.

Problem: Too many places to look for a particular piece of paper.

Solution: You are probably using too many hanging folders and too many file folders. Look at your file folders and see which ones could be grouped together in one hanging folder. Don't start a separate file folder until you have accumulated five to eight pages of related information. Until that point, group papers with others.

Problem: After taking a file out, you don't know where it belongs.

Solution: This is less likely to occur if you keep hanging folders in the file cabinet and take out only the file folder. If you're still having trouble, make sure you keep a thorough index of your files. It may also help to color coordinate your file folders so that all folders in one file drawer are the same color.

Problem: Losing papers between hanging folders.

Solution: Make sure you use file folders within hanging folders and always place your papers in a file folder. Some hanging folders are a lighter color inside to help you see that you are placing a file inside, rather than outside, the hanging folder. There are also connectors available that join one hanging folder to another, making it impossible to lose papers between hanging folders.

Problem: You need to have personal files accessible, but you can't free up an entire file drawer for them.

Solution: Get another file cabinet (or vertical file holder, or file cart). Don't put personal papers in the same file drawer as your work-related papers.

Problem: The file drawer is too full and you can't move the folders back and forth in order to take file folders out.

Solution: Weed out files and leave about an inch leeway in the file drawer so the folders have room to move.

Problem: You have to shuffle through the folder to find the most current papers.

Solution: Keep the most recent papers in front where they are readily available.

Toward a paperless business environment

For years there has been talk of a "paperless society." It looks as if we won't be paperless for a while, not because of the technology needed (it exists), but because of our habits. If you're willing to change the way you work, technology can help you further reduce the papers in your office.

Electronic Mail

Electronic mail (e-mail) eliminates the need for standard memos and many times business letters, as a way of conveying information. Although the purpose of e-mail is to transmit information quickly, eliminating the need for paper, many business professionals insist on printing out hard-copy versions.

There are a few ways to make e-mail more effective:

- Don't get in the habit of saving and printing every e-mail you receive. If you know you'll never refer to an e-mail message again, dump it. If you want to keep an e-mail indefinitely, save it to a CD, Zip or other type of backup labeled "e-mail."

- When sending messages to multiple recipients, keep everyone's e-mail addresses private by using the Blind Carbon Copy (BCC) feature of your e-mail program.

- Be concise. If you can use fewer words, use them (or spare them).

- Make sure you're not on everyone's distribution list. If you are, ask to be removed immediately.

- Take the time to clear out old e-mail messages that you know you'll never refer to again and keep the important messages stored electronically.

Scanners

There are handheld, sheet-fed, flatbed, and optical pen scanners available to reduce the amount of papers in your office. A scanner will help you in several ways:

- If you need to import a document or graphic that is not already a computer file, a scanner will digitalize the information (turn it into a computer file).

- If you want to minimize your paper files, you can convert them to computer documents then toss the piece of paper.

- If you use graphics for advertisements, brochures or other reasons, scanners will convert them to computer files.

Shredders

The convenience of shredders is second only to the safety aspect. Identity theft and company knowledge theft is rampant. So while you're shredding papers to make room for more information, you can take comfort in knowing that the information you're tossing won't fall into the wrong hands.

> The quickest way to eliminate the paper in your office without filling endless trash bags, is to shred everything.

If you need to see pieces of paper in front of you, rather than read your information on a computer screen, it's important that you learn how to efficiently handle the paper that continually flows into your home office. This is why the next chapter is devoted to handling incoming information.

Handling Incoming Information Efficiently

10

Handling Incoming Information Efficiently

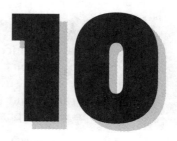

Some papers, such as mail, magazines, business cards, newspapers, and books, fall somewhere between current and reference. Many people find that this is the most difficult type of information to categorize. That's why it usually ends up in stacks on, next to, or around your desk.

A real estate agent at one of my seminars admitted that he used to be so overwhelmed by the volume of his incoming mail that he just let it accumulate everywhere. Magazines, letters, and newspapers were scattered all over his office. One day he returned home to find police searching through his office. His mother-in-law, who had come to visit, had taken a look at his office and was certain he'd been robbed.

> Before bringing anything into your home office, throw out any mail you know you'll never look at again. This alone will cut down on clutter tremendously.

The best way to deal with mail is to spend a few minutes each day processing it. This means taking the time to open each envelope, make a decision on it (remember P-A-P-E-R: put it in a stacking bin, act on it, put it in a file, enter it on your To-Do list and file it, or rid yourself of it), and move on to the next piece.

Using a postal service

A good way to reduce the amount of information that comes into your home is to pick up your business mail elsewhere. Using a mail service center such as *Mail Boxes, Etc.*, makes it easy to keep your business and personal mail separate. There are other advantages to using a postal center:

- You can sort through your mail while you're there and take home only the information you need.

- No one will know your home address, which will keep clients and salespeople from showing up at your door.

- A street address along with a number sign and number gives a more professional impression than a post office box number. Some people are wary of a business that has a post office box number in its address

- The postal service will accept packages for you and sign for them, while some delivery services won't deliver to a post office box.

- A postal service allows you to mail packages by overnight express, send and receive fax transmissions, make copies, and send packages by various means.

The disadvantages are that you have to drive somewhere to get your mail, and there's a small overcharge when you buy stamps from a postal service instead of directly from the post office.

A note about postal suites. Postal fraud committed by individuals using postal suite addresses to give the appearance of a leased office, has changed government regulations. Now all postal center box holders must substitute a # sign for the word "suite" or use PMB (postal mail box) before their box number.

Mail handling tips

As technology increases and marketers discover electronic ways to market and advertise to consumers, junk mail will decrease. For the time being, though, junk mail isn't going away. Neither is important and necessary mail from clients, creditors and family. To deal with the constant flow of mail coming into your office, I recommend that you do the following:

1) Take the mail straight to your office instead of opening it elsewhere in your home. When you open mail at your desk, you'll reduce the risk of losing important papers, it will be easier for you to make decisions, and you'll easily be able to put the sorted mail where it belongs.

2) Designate one place, preferably your **To Sort** bin, for all of your incoming mail. You could use a wicker basket kept near or under your desk, or stacking trays kept on a file cabinet. Choose a spot other than your desktop. Don't use an "In basket" on your desk, because it will fill up quickly with unsorted material, and that leads to unnecessary distractions.

3) Always open your mail at the same place, at your desk and next to a wastebasket.

> Opening your mail next to the wastebasket makes it easier to throw out right away what you don't need.

4) Open all of your mail at one sitting. This takes a few minutes, but saves time in the long run. Open each piece of mail, make a decision about it, and move on to the next piece. If you stop to make a phone call or to do something else, this process will take longer than it needs to. When your mind is set on a task, that task will be completed sooner if you stay focused on it.

5) Read each piece of mail long enough to know what action is required and by what date. If you don't bother to read invitations, notices, and announcements, you may miss out on various meetings and time-sensitive opportunities.

6) Make as many decisions right away as you can. If you put something aside "until later," you've already made the decision not to decide.

7) Throw out any unnecessary papers, envelopes, and enclosures and save only the vital documents you need.

8) A fast way to respond to certain types of correspondence is to write a note at the bottom of the letter and send it back. Many people would rather receive a prompt response written at the bottom of a letter than a delayed, formal response. If you want to keep a record of this correspondence, all you have to do is photocopy this sheet of paper.

9) Remember to record on your To-Do list any action you need to take before you file any papers away. If you put papers in your current files without making a note of them, you're no better off than you were when your papers were in stacks all over your desk.

The only way to be in control of your mail is to handle it on a regular basis and to get into the habit of making immediate decisions on each piece. At that point, you may actually look forward to getting the mail.

Keep in mind that your name is being bought and sold on a regular basis. If you order merchandise by mail, you are a prime candidate to receive many mail order catalogues. To cut down on the volume of this type of mail you receive, send a letter to the Direct Marketing Association and request that your name be removed from mail order lists:

> Mail Preference Service
>
> c/o DMA
>
> P.O. Box 9008
>
> Farmingdale, NY 11735-9008

How to deal with magazines

We are a society that generates endless amounts of information. There is a magazine for almost any interest, from scuba diving to stamp collecting. Some are hard to resist, and you may end up subscribing to too many. When that happens, you run out of time to read them all.

> It's important for you to realize that it is simply not possible for you to read everything you would like to read.

When your magazines start to accumulate, your level of guilt over not reading them increases proportionately. When you take that pressure off yourself, you can become more selective about what you read. To lessen your guilt, and your stacks of magazines, I recommend that you do the following:

1) Limit the number of subscription magazines you receive. When a subscription comes up for renewal, take this opportunity to determine whether or not you regularly read it. Keep in mind that if you ever need to refer to an article, you can retrieve it online or order back issues from the publisher.

2) Keep your personal magazines stored in one place with other personal magazines and catalogues, preferably somewhere other than your home office.

3) Keep your professional magazines in your **To Read** stacking bin or another designated spot until you are ready to read them. Absolutely keep them off your desk and out of the way of your papers in progress.

4) Go through your reading bin once a week and tear out the articles you will read at a later date. Put these articles in a folder labeled **To Read** and keep the folder in the bin or in your briefcase if you use it daily. When you leave for an appointment, grab the folder and go. After you've read an article, either throw it away, put it in your **To File** bin, or file it.

5) If you don't want to rip up your magazines, make copies of the articles you want to read. Then file the magazines in a magazine holder labeled with the name of the magazine and the year.

> When you file magazines, put a detachable note on the outside cover listing the articles you may need to refer to later.

6) Another alternative is to highlight on the magazine's table of contents the articles you want to read. Keep the magazine in your **To Read** bin until you have a chance to get to it. As you read the article, highlight the important parts for reference later.

7) Keep only a year's worth of magazines. When the new year starts, replace the first issue you stored with the new issue. Remember, the library has plenty of room to store magazines. For catalogues, keep only one season's worth. When you get a second, throw away the first.

8) Purchase magazines on CD or subscribe to online publications. Many publications offer the alternative of receiving a CD instead of the magazine. Instead of stacks of magazines, you'll have a few CDs.

Sturdy plastic file boxes can be used to organize magazines and catalogues. (Courtesy of Esselte Corporation)

QUICK TIP FOR HOME OFFICE PROFESSIONALS

Set aside time each week to read. Schedule it on your calendar. Even spending half an hour or an hour each morning reading makes a big difference in getting through all of the newspapers, professional publications, sales information, brochures, and other material you need to read.

How to deal with newspapers

Newspapers are short-lived—they're history after a few days. Yet so many people hold onto them until they get the opportunity to read them. If you haven't read the newspapers stacked in your home office (or kitchen, or another part of your house) after three days, toss them or recycle them. The following are a few tips to help you save time handling newspapers:

1) Determine whether you should continue receiving the newspaper. You can do this quickly by looking at your newspaper recycling pile. If all, or almost all, of the daily newspapers are unread, cancel your subscription and buy the paper only on Sunday. If newspapers only distract you from working, cancel your subscription.

2) When you receive the newspaper, bring it into your home office (if no one else will be reading it), take out the sections you plan to read, and put them in your **To Read** bin. Then get rid of the rest of the paper.

3) When you go through the paper, cut out any articles you want to keep. If someone else will be reading the paper after you, place a check mark next to the articles you want to save, and when the other reader is through, cut them out. You'll save time searching for these articles by making a note on the front page of the section where an article is located.

4) After you've cut out an article, write on the right-hand corner where it will be filed. If it's an article you would like to keep for some time, make a photocopy of the original because the original will eventually yellow.

5) As you read an article, highlight the points you will refer to again. When you go back to the article, you'll be able to go right to the "meat" of it.

6) Consider replacing your newspaper with immediate, online news from one of several online services. You will get straight news, without all of the extra features and advertising.

How to handle business cards

Business cards are a blessing because they're an easy and inexpensive way to market your home-based business, but they become a curse when the business cards you receive in return start to accumulate. You can either refuse to accept them, keep them in a drawer with a rubber band around them, or organize them. While electronically entering information from business cards is the fastest and easiest way to handle business cards, it's not the only way.

A card holder is an efficient way to file business cards. When cards are stored vertically in a holder, they're easy to flip through. There are a variety of products you may want to use in conjunction with your card file:

- Consider buying clear or colored plastic sleeves that fit over the business cards and attach to the bottom of the card file.

- There is a punch available that strategically places two holes in a business card to allow you to file it quickly. This way you don't have to copy the information on a blank card and store the original elsewhere. This also beats cutting and attaching a business card by hand.

- Another product—a plastic adhesive strip with holes in it—attaches to the bottom of a business card so you can file it directly in the card file.

- If you have a 3" x 5" card file—larger than business card size—staple or tape a business card to the left-hand side of a card, leaving space on the right-hand side for personal information about the person (e.g., the administrative assistant's name, a spouse's name, birthdays).

When you file a business card, you can file it under either the name of the business or the name of the individual. Choose whichever approach will come to your mind first when you need to retrieve the information.

When copying information onto a blank file card, put the phone number in the upper right-hand corner of the card to make it easy to see. You have to push the file open further to read a number written at the bottom of a card.

Keep business cards you receive while traveling in an envelope in your personal planner or in an envelope stashed where you'll find it when you return to your office. Then file them when you get home.

Save business cards that need to be filed in the front of your card file or in a small container next to your card file. Then file them once a week. In addition to a business card file for your desk, there are other options that might work well for you:

- A business card book, available in 8 1/2" x 11" or smaller, keeps business cards stored in plastic sleeves. It's not practical to alphabetize the cards throughout the book, because each time you get a new business card you have to move every card. Instead, keep a page for the A's, one for the B's, and so on. Then alphabetize the cards within each page. Or you can store the cards by category (for example, by region of the country, by supplier, or by the service offered).

- Do you have phone numbers listed in your card file, daily planner or computer? Are clients' business cards stuffed in a desk drawer? Organize names, addresses and phone numbers by entering them in a contact management program. Such programs as "ACT!" and "Goldmine" offer more features than a calendar program, including a place for names, addresses and phone numbers. You can still take this contact information with you by printing it onto sheets that fit in a standard daily planner or reducing the 8 1/2" x 11" sheets by 64 percent. After you enter the information from a business card, throw away the card and eliminate duplicate information.

- Contact management software is an efficient way to store client contact information. Before you leave town, you just print out the names you need and keep the updated list with you in your planner or briefcase. If you reduce the list to fit your planner, it is extremely convenient

> A timesaving option is to use a business card scanner that quickly transfers information from a business card to your computer.

to use. If you take your laptop with you everywhere, don't print your list and use your laptop instead.

Computerizing your business card information saves space because you don't need to keep the original business cards once the information is entered in your computer.

- Handheld organizers offer a quick way for entering and accessing client information. You can either enter this information manually or transfer data from your contact management software program. When you need a phone number you don't have to wait for your computer to boot up and could even use your PDA to place the call.

By storing contact information from business cards electronically, you create only one place for storing up-to-date contact information. Otherwise you may have contact information stored in your planner, card file, computer and handheld, yet not all synchronized.

Debbie, a sales rep, was away from her home office from Monday through Friday, three weeks out of each month. Because she was rarely home, she had to keep all of her clients' names with her at all times. She was constantly updating her client list by hand, to the point where she could hardly read it. Each time she acquired a new client, she would transfer the information from her client's card to her list. She kept telling herself that she would rewrite her list, but she never found the time to do it. I suggested that she use a computer program to keep her list up to date.

Now when Debbie meets a new client, she enters his or her name in her notebook computer and has those names with her always. To avoid duplicating information, she throws away business cards after she has entered the information. On weekends when she is home, Debbie backs up her notebook and synchronizes it with your desktop. Her second option was to start using a PDA, but Debbie didn't want to part with her notebook computer.

> Go through your business card file or computerized contact list at least twice a year and remove the cards or names you no longer need.

Keeping books under control

To many people, being in a bookstore is like being in a candy store—there are so many to choose from, and you want them all.

Before you buy a book, ask yourself why you want it. Are you buying it because it's a best-seller and you know everyone will be talking about it, or does it deal with a topic that interests you? Will it increase your income or just distract you when you should be working? The following are some tips on keeping your books under control:

- Go through the books you own now and pull out any you know you won't read, then give them away or sell them. Bookstores throughout the country buy used books. You won't earn much money, but you'll gain much-needed space in your office.

- Check books out of the library instead of buying them. In addition to saving money, you'll have an incentive to read the book before it's due back. When you check out a book, make a note in your daily planner a few days before the due date to give yourself a chance to finish it.

- Listen to books on tape. This is a good way to save time while keeping up on the latest books. You could listen to them while you are in your office, in your car, or exercising.

> There are companies that summarize on tape the books you want to read but don't have time to read.

- Buy e-books (electronic books available online). You could download a book to your notebook and read between appointments or while traveling.

- Invest in a sturdy bookcase. If your books are out of sight, they'll definitely be out of mind, and you'll never read or even refer to them. Arrange books on your bookcase (1) alphabetically by author, (2) alphabetically by title in general categories (e.g., business, personal, motivational), or (3) alphabetically by title according to subject (e.g., sales, marketing, computers).

- You can distinguish categories of books by putting a different colored dot on the spine of each one. If you file your books alphabetically by author, refiling is easy if you use a different colored dot for each letter of the alphabet. If you file your books by general category or subject, use a different color for each one. When a book covers several areas, put a colored dot on the spine for each area.

- When you read a book, highlight a point you want to remember. Use a highlighter pen that doesn't bleed through to the next page. Then add a word at the top of the page to take you to that place. Another option is to use a detachable note that sticks out of the edge of the book.

Operating a home office involves a lot of expenses, from printing to postage. Spending the money is easy. Keeping track of where you've spent it is a challenge. In the next chapter, you'll learn ways to track your expenses that will save you many frustrating hours at tax time.

QUICK TIP FOR HOME OFFICE PROFESSIONALS

Streamline wherever you can. If something serves no purpose, simplify. If you don't know where to store something that you won't use anyway, simplify. The less you have to deal with both mentally and physically, the more you can enjoy the items you know you'll use and the activities you enjoy doing.

- Toss out any papers you can.

- Move paper forward each time you handle it.

- Drop meaningless tasks from your To-Do list.

- Learn the fine art of ignoring problems that will solve themselves or will never be solved.

- Minimize the time you spend looking for things.

- Use it or lose it. Anything you don't use doesn't belong in your office.

Organizing Receipts

Organizing Receipts

Most people stash their receipts in a shoebox throughout the year and deal with them near tax time or before the deadline their accountant gives them. The inconvenience comes when it's time to sort through the receipts and prepare your tax return. Instead of spending time on your business, you have to take a day or a week to divide your receipts, to make sure they are properly recorded, and to total them.

> Receipts come in many sizes, from small cash register receipts to large invoices.

Whether you own your own business or are a corporate employee in a home office, you will need to pay taxes. Keeping track of your receipts will ensure that you get all of the deductions to which you are entitled. If you are a corporate employee, you will be reimbursed for the amount of money you spend on company expenses.

Natalie, a computer programmer who attended one of my seminars, was transferred from a corporate office to her home. After two years of working at home, she added up all of the money she had spent on office supplies and discovered that her receipts totaled $450. Realizing that this represented serious money, she belatedly turned in her receipts, and was refused reimbursement because she'd had them for so long. If she had been in control of her receipts sooner, she would have been $450 richer. If you're an entrepreneur, you will want to do the following:

- Keep track of all of your expenses in order to document how company money was spent.

- Use most of your receipts at the end of the year in preparation for your tax return.

- Maintain receipts so you can produce the ones you claimed as deductions if you are audited.

If you're a corporate employee, you will want to do the following:

- Keep track of your expenses so that you can be reimbursed by your employer.

- Use only a few receipts at the end of the year in preparing your tax return, depending upon how many were reimbursed.

- Be able to obtain reimbursement and expense records from the corporate office were you to be audited.

QUICK TIP FOR HOME OFFICE PROFESSIONALS

Keep one credit card for business expenses and one for personal expenses. This way there will be no question about whether an item was a business or personal expense.

Keeping track of receipts

Doing your taxes should not be a long, drawn out process. If you take the time to organize your receipts during the year, you'll see at least three benefits.

1) You'll shorten the amount of time you spend preparing your taxes.

2) If you use an accountant, you'll significantly reduce your bill, as he will spend less time sorting through your receipts. If your accountant has to look through hundreds of receipts, your bill will be tremendous.

3) You'll be able to see throughout the year how much money you're spending.

During the day, keep an envelope with you at all times to hold receipts from business expenses you incur. On meal receipts, be sure to write the name of the person, company, title, type of meal, and reason for the meeting. Then, at least once a week, process these receipts by entering their amounts in your accounting program and filing them away. It's unrealistic to think that you will be able to enter your receipts daily. Instead, keep them in a folder labeled **Receipts to Enter**.

After you've entered your expenses, there are a few ways you can store receipts to prevent them from becoming a major nuisance and to minimize the time it takes to organize them for tax purposes. Whatever method you choose, the key is to keep your receipts under control by keeping them in a specific place so that you'll be able to organize them at tax time with the least amount of time and effort. It's important to choose a receipt filing system with which you are comfortable, and to keep it as simple as possible. The more difficult it is to use, the less likely you will be to use it. If handling finances is not your strength, hire a bookkeeper to track your finances and manage your receipts. The amount of money you spend on a bookkeeper will be considerably less than the amount of time you would waste trying to handle your own records.

Using files

When you store your receipts in files, they are readily accessible. Even more important, you can file them by main categories and subcategories. This is helpful when you're preparing a tax return because all of your receipts will already be broken down by subcategory. It's also helpful when you need to track down a specific receipt, because you won't have to look through all of your receipts to find it.

Hanging folders work well to file your receipts because they accommodate file folders for the subcategories you select.

> One method for filing receipts is by category.

Another option is to use expandable (accordion) folders.

The following are tips for using a categorical filing system for your receipts:

1) Label hanging folders with your main categories (for example, Car).

2) Label file folders with your subcategories (for example, Insurance, Maintenance, and Mileage) and place them in the hanging folders.

3) Each time you get a receipt, place it in the appropriate folder after entering it in your accounting program.

4) At the end of the year, take the receipts out of each file folder, staple them together by category, and store them in a manila envelope. Label the envelope **Taxes** and include the year. You'll use your computer printout by category to complete your tax return.

Another option is to file your receipts by month. This system works better if you'll have only a few receipts each month. Otherwise, a monthly system makes it difficult to locate an individual receipt because you have to hunt through all of the files until you find the receipt you need.

Using accordion folders

The accordion folder system works much the same way as the file system, but the receipts are stored in an accordion folder instead of a file.

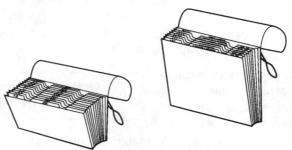

Accordion folders keep your receipts organized and accessible. (Courtesy of Globe-Weis)

Set up this system as follows:

1) Start with an accordion folder. (If possible, use one that isn't preprinted with letters or numbers.)

2) Label as many sections inside the accordion folder as you think you'll need. Label each section with a main category (for example, Office Supplies, Postage, Car).

Computerized recordkeeping

The amount of paperwork involved in accounting keeps many people from bothering with balancing their books, entering receipts and ultimately completing their tax returns until the last minute. Take advantage of the many business accounting software programs available to simplify the record keeping process. There are definitely benefits to using a computerized system.

- There is less room for error because you aren't doing all of the arithmetic.

- There is no paper involved until you print out your end-of-the-year statement.

- At any time you can tell how much you are spending and under what category.

If computerized recordkeeping interests you, take the time to investigate the various business accounting software programs available. Before investing in a program, determine the following:

- What do you want and need the program to do? You'll waste money on a program designed for a large business when you or your partner are the only employees.

- Is the program easy to use and is there technical support available?

- Will the program continue to meet your needs in a few years? If not, buy a program with capabilities you will use in the future.

After you select and install a personal finance program, do the following:

- Limit the number of categories you set up. If you make your system unnecessarily complicated, it defeats your intentions, which is to simplify your life.

- After you pay your bills using your business accounting program, enter the check number, amount, name or company to whom you wrote the check and which category it fits into. It's a good idea to enter receipts as you pay your bills. (Paying bills online is a good way to save time and eliminate extra paperwork.)

- Handle the receipts you receive while out of your office by either entering the receipts on your computer when you return to your office, or filing them in folders by month and at the end of the month entering all of your receipts.

- Don't forget that you'll still need a method for storing receipts. Any of the methods previously mentioned will work for you.

- Remember to keep at least one backup copy of your electronic records.

Sample categories for filing receipts

Use the following categories as a guide when setting up your receipt filing system. Use hanging folders for main categories and file folders for subcategories. If you chose a filing system that doesn't make use of main categories, use just the main categories.

Hanging Folder	File Folder
Administrative Expenses	Office Supplies
	Postage
	Printing
Automobile Expenses	Maintenance
	Mileage

Hanging Folder	File Folder
Client Expenses	Gifts
	Meals and Entertainment
Contributions	Charitable Contributions
	Donated Merchandise
Education	Association Dues
	Seminars
	Classes
Home Office	Rent or House Payment
	Repairs
Insurance	Car
	Home
	Life
	Medical
Interest on Loans	Bank Loans
	Charge Accounts
	Office Equipment
	Small Business Association
Investments	Pension and Profit-Sharing
	SEP Contributions
Invoices	A-D or Client A
	E-H or Client B
	I-L or Client C
	M-P
	Q-Z

Hanging Folder	File Folder
Marketing	Advertising
	Marketing
Miscellaneous	Laundry and Cleaning
	Legal and Professional Fees
Operating Expenses	Equipment Purchases/Leasing
	Long-Distance Calls
	Safe Deposit Box Rental
Travel Expenses	Airfare
	Car Rental
	Lodging
Utilities	Electric
	Gas
	Water

Which documents do you need to keep and for how long?

During my seminars I am often asked about what receipts or documentation a home office professional needs to keep and for how long. The general statute of limitations for the Internal Revenue Service is three years. However, this varies from state to state. The IRS can go back as far as seven years and, if they suspect fraud, they may go back as far as they like. I recommend that you keep your canceled checks and tax return information for seven years. If you are still unsure about what to keep, contact your local IRS office and your certified public accountant (CPA).

After you have completed your income tax form, make a copy of it. Mail the original to the government, and keep your copy—with all of your documentation and receipts—in a manila envelope. If all of this information doesn't fit, use an accordion file. Store past returns in a storage box, separated by year, and label the outside of the box.

Tips for dealing with the Internal Revenue Service

You can help avoid problems with the Internal Revenue Service (IRS) by keeping thorough records of your business expenses and by understanding business deductions and their limitations. For example, if you are claiming a portion of your home for business use, make sure that the room is being used for business purposes only. A foldout bed in your office will prevent you from being able to legitimately claim that room for business use exclusively.

If you are audited, you want to be helpful and accommodating to the IRS auditor, but you also don't want to pay any more taxes than you have to. With this in mind, the following are tips for handling the auditing process:

1) If you are audited, bring representation with you (your CPA or bookkeeper). They know how to deal with the IRS and will have a good idea of the questions the IRS will ask you.

2) If you go alone to the audit, do not automatically answer every question you are asked. If, for example, the auditor asks you how much you spent on gasoline last year and you don't know, it's okay to tell the auditor that you will find out and let him or her know. If you make a guess and it's incorrect, that information may be used against you.

3) Don't panic. If you've kept good records while you've been in business, you shouldn't have anything to worry about. If you haven't, keep good records, it's never too late to start. An audit could provide just the motivation you've needed.

Using a certified public accountant

Hiring a CPA is one of the best investments you can make. You'll save yourself time in preparing taxes and, more important, you'll protect yourself to a certain degree from being audited by the IRS. The following tips will make it easier for you to work with your CPA:

1) Make your tax information easy for your CPA to understand.

2) Rather than hand your CPA a shoebox full of receipts, separate the receipts, record the totals for each category, and give your accountant the totals. If you've set up a system for handling receipts as described earlier, all you have to do is total the expenses. Your CPA does not need to see your individual receipts, but you do need to hold onto them in the event that you are audited.

3) If you're missing receipts for items you charged, give your CPA a copy of your charge card statements, with the tax-deductible charges highlighted and the type of expense explained. Some credit card companies prepare a year-end summary for you.

How to save bank statements and cancelled checks

You'll save time at tax time if you handle your bank statements and canceled checks just once, at the end of the month. It's a good idea to keep a separate checking account for business expenses. This way there is no confusion about which expenses are personal and which are work-related, either in your mind or in the mind of the IRS.

You don't need to store banking deposit slips. You do, however, need to set up a system for storing bank statements and canceled checks. For these you have three options: binders, folders, or accordion files.

> Keep banking deposit slips only until you have checked them off the next monthly bank statement.

The Binder Method

1) Reconcile your account either electronically or manually.

2) Store the bank statements in a three-ring binder labeled with the year.

3) Keep the canceled checks in a small accordion file labeled either by month or by category of expense.

How you file your canceled checks depends upon how your mind works. If you need to find a canceled check and the only thing you remember is the type of expense (not the date), storing your canceled checks categorically will make it easier for you to find the checks you need.

The File Method

1) Label a hanging folder Bank/Checks.

2.) Label a file folder Bank Statements and file your statements there.

3) Label more file folders either with the names of your expense categories or with the names of the month. File your canceled checks in them. Depending on the number of checks you write each month, you may want to use a box-bottom folder.

The Accordion File Method

1) Use an accordion file labeled by month and store the entire statement within the corresponding month.

2) At the end of each year, label the accordion folder and file it with your tax returns.

Tips for making tax time easier

1) Document the miles you drive for business purposes.

2) Remember to send 1099 forms to any entity to which you have made payments of $600 or more (i.e., consultants or contractors). If you don't, you'll have to pay a penalty.

3) Don't wait until a few days before April 15 to turn in your tax information to your accountant. This does not give your accountant enough time to complete your return before the tax deadline.

4) Keep a list of your stocks, CDs, and money market accounts so that you'll know what statements you need at the end of the year. If you forget to report information about these accounts, you'll have to pay penalties.

5) After you've filed your return, store copies of your return and supporting documents in manila envelopes clearly labeled by year. Store all of this documentation in a sturdy box (with a lid) and labeled with the appropriate span of years.

6) Then store the box in an out-of-the-way place, such as your garage or attic. If you have the space, another option is to store your returns in a file cabinet (preferably one that locks).

> If you store boxes in your garage, place them on pallets to keep them dry.

How to maintain your sanity before tax time

April 15th approaches quickly each year. If at the beginning of April, you haven't finished your taxes, you can panic or take action.

- Gather all of your receipts from your drawers, pockets, and folders and divide them by category. An easy way to determine which categories you'll need are to use last year's tax return as a guide.

- If you've installed an accounting program on your computer, learned how to use it but never found time to enter your receipts, start now. Even if you're familiar with the program but haven't used it, take a few minutes to set up your categories and in the end you'll have a printout of what your expenses were by category.

- Either transfer the totals from the expenses sheet to your tax forms, finish your calculations and mail your taxes, or give the sheet to your accountant (if he or she will still do your taxes this late).

- If you're doing your calculations manually, separate your receipts by category and start tackling each pile. Using a reliable calculator, add your expenses by category, enter the totals and either complete your taxes or give your accountant the totals. Don't bother giving him your receipts or financial statements. Instead, store them in a safe place.

- If after sorting through your receipts, financial statements and other documents (including 1099's), you realize that you'll never finish your taxes on time or are missing documents, your best bet is to file an extension. It's better to complete your return correctly and late, than riddled with errors and on time. Along with your extension, don't forget to include a check to the IRS for the taxes (you think you owe) on your net taxable income. The extension will give you until August 15th to complete and mail your taxes.

- If you file an extension, remember to include self-employment tax (if applicable) and if you're paying estimated taxes, your first quarterly payment is also due on April 15th.

Keeping track of your receipts on a regular basis is one of those tasks that people often put aside because they "don't have time." The tips in the following chapter should help you gain better control over how you use your time so that routine matters don't turn into organizational nightmares.

Making Better Use of Your Time

Making Better Use of Your Time

Winston Churchill said, "Time is one thing that can never be retrieved. One may lose and regain a friend, one may lose and regain money, opportunity once spurned may come again, but the hours that are lost in idleness can never be brought back to be used in gainful pursuits."

To see how much time you are wasting that could be spent on gainful pursuits, you need to track your activities for an entire day. Using the chart on page 214, do this for one day this week, and then do it for another day next week. After you've taken the time to record and analyze how you're spending your time, you can then work to eliminate those activities that are time wasters or to reschedule tasks so that your time is used more efficiently.

If you find it difficult to get excited about the idea of tracking your activities for a day, think about how nice it would be to have enough time to finish that project you're working on, or to start that project you've been talking about, or even to take some time off for once. The key to accomplishing more is to make better use of the hours you have available each day.

Evaluating Your Use Of Time

Activities

	Starting Time	Ending Time	Total Time Spent
7:00 a.m.			
8:00			
9:00			
10:00			
11:00			
12:00 p.m.			
1:00			
2:00			
3:00			
4:00			
5:00			
6:00			

©Lisa Kanarek, HomeOfficeLife.com

How to make better use of your time

Time management is an overused and misunderstood term. It's not possible to control time. There are only 24 hours in each day and 168 hours in each week. It is possible, however, to control what you do with your time. Making better use of your time will help you overcome the feeling that you're running in place—you have a list a mile long, and no matter how hard you work, you never seem to accomplish as much as you should.

Throughout the day, ask yourself if what you are doing is the best use of your time. Every few hours, stop what you're doing and decide if the task you're working on is the one that needs to be done today or if it is one that could be done at a later date. You don't have to check up on yourself more often than every three hours. Frequent checks would be disruptive. Set the alarm on your watch, or set a timer to go off, or set the alarm on your computer if you're going to be home most of the day.

Some people jump out of bed at 5:00 each morning and are ready to go, whereas others aren't able to function well until the afternoon. Concentrate on important tasks during the time you're most productive. Leave the less important tasks for when your energy level is low.

> Determine your best time of day and schedule important tasks for that time.

Stay focused on the activity at hand. Many of us tend to start one project and then bounce to another without finishing the first. At the end of the day, it's possible to feel exhausted without having accomplished anything. The problem is a lack of focus. When you focus on the project you're working on, you can complete it faster.

Kristine, a sales rep for a gift company, was excited about finally organizing her home office. As we worked together on organizing her desk drawers, she would start on one, then jump to another, then skip to a third. I persuaded Kristine to get back to the first drawer, and after that we started getting somewhere. When we were finished, we had a little talk about using time wisely. Kristine's misguided enthusiasm had helped me see how she had gotten so disorganized in the first place.

Schedule at least one full day a week in the office. If you spend a majority of your time out of the office, set aside one day to spend in your office catching up on paperwork, making phone calls, and planning the following week. Determine which day of the week is slower for you in terms of phone calls you receive or appointments you make, and make that the day you spend in your office. You may have to make an effort to keep that day clear, but if you do, the rest of your week will go more smoothly.

Make appointments with yourself to work on certain tasks. Treat yourself as you would a client, and put yourself on your calendar. Block out certain time periods when you will work on specific tasks. The task could be a monthly report, a client proposal, or a marketing plan—something that needs to be done and that needs your full attention. Treat this time as an appointment to keep, and make it a productive session. During this time, turn on your answering machine and concentrate only on the project you've scheduled. If you wait for an "opportune moment" to work on projects, it will never come.

Learn to say no. Do you have trouble saying no? When you don't set limits, the quality of your work suffers and your ability to maintain quality service is reduced. You end up disappointing the clients you didn't want to turn away. There's nothing wrong with being busy, until the quality of your service suffers.

Denise, a bank consultant, had so much to do that she started missing deadlines. Her home-based business had grown more quickly than she'd anticipated, but she didn't want to turn down any new clients. Soon, she was losing clients. She decided to stop taking on more projects than she had time to complete and to concentrate on accomplishing her top-priority tasks first. Although it hurts to turn down work, clients are much more understanding about your being busy than they are about your missing deadlines.

Keep like with like. Group similar items so that you'll be able to find what you need immediately. File related paperwork in the same place so that you'll have fewer places to look for it. When things are scattered around your office, you end up spending more time looking for them.

It's also a good idea to group similar tasks. Run all of your calls at once so that you don't keep interrupting your work time with phone calls all day. Answer e-mails during another block of time. You'll find that they get done more quickly if you do several at once because you are able to fully concentrate on that particular type of task. When you're scheduling appointments, group them with other appointments. Schedule appointments in the same area at the same time, and avoid making two trips where one might do. Do all of your errands in one afternoon, instead of taking a bit of time out of every afternoon. The more you group like tasks and like items together, the more efficiently you'll be using your time.

Have a place for everything. By now you know that your office should have "a place for everything, and everything in its place." Don't put things anywhere "for now," or they may end up there forever. Designate a specific place for the papers and supplies you need on a regular basis and remember to store the same types of items together. You will spend less time searching for lost items and more time accomplishing important tasks.

Take the extra few seconds to put something away where it belongs, instead of putting it near the place it belongs. Rather than putting it at the top of the basement stairs or by the door leading to the garage, take the extra minute to put it away properly. The greater number of times you handle an item before you put it away, the more time you waste.

Keep frequently used items in reach and in stock. Remember the work circle, and keep the items you use on a regular basis within arm's reach. Even though your office may be small, each time you have to leave your desk to get something, you waste valuable time. You also leave yourself open to distractions. While you're on your way to the place you store extra supplies, you may find something else to do.

Keep track of supplies that are running low, as was discussed in Chapter 4. If you don't have enough stamps to mail your letters, or paper to print your proposal, or letterhead to print letters, you'll end up wasting time while you scramble to obtain what you need.

Hire outside help if necessary. Personal service businesses continue to grow as demands on our time increase. Small business owners often don't want to

> It's easier to hire someone on a project-by-project basis than to bring someone on full time.

hire additional people full time, so they opt for freelancers.

There comes a point when you'll realize that you can't do everything yourself. Whether the task is entering information into your computer, running errands, cleaning your house, or answering the phone, it's often better to hire someone to do it for you. A good way to decide if it's worth hiring someone to handle a task is to multiply your hourly rate by the number of hours you estimate the task will take. If your time could be better spent on projects and tasks that would generate income for your business, bring someone in to do the routine tasks that have to be done.

Arnold, a marketing consultant, needed to enter over 1,500 names in his computer. He kept putting off the chore because of the amount of time it would take to do it. Finally he hired a high school student to enter the names. Instead of spending his time typing, he was out of his office consulting at an hourly rate that easily covered the cost of hiring the high school student.

Some people feel it takes more time to explain how to do something than to do it themselves. Although it does take time to train someone to help you, the initial investment you make in training someone will save time in the long run. Hiring the right person will help speed this process, and so will making sure you train this person effectively.

Matthew, a freelance editor, wanted the tasks he delegated done as quickly as possible, so he would rush through his instructions. Then he would get upset when the result wasn't what he wanted. He even had trouble delegating to his children. He asked his young daughter to put the clothes in the dryer, which she did. But he didn't say anything about turning the dryer on, so she didn't. We worked on Matthew's delegating skills, and now he does the following:

- He clearly describes what he wants done.
- He asks the person to repeat his instructions back to him.
- He sets clear deadlines for completion.
- He follows up on the progress of delegated tasks.

Now Matthew finds that the projects he delegates are completed correctly and on time, leaving him with more time to work on important projects.

Allocate a few minutes at the end of each day to put away papers, clear your desk, and plan for the next day. It takes only a few minutes of "maintenance" each day to save you valuable time in the long run. Think in terms of laundry. If you let it pile up for weeks, you'll create a problem, and you'll have to spend hours washing clothes. If you wash your clothes every few days, laundry won't be a problem.

At the end of the day, take a few minutes to "close out" the day. Thursday evening, get ready for Friday. That way you won't have to face Thursday's mess when you walk in the door Friday morning. If you had a hectic day, you surely don't want to relive it the next day.

A sales rep in one of my audiences told us that the minute he opened the door to his home office, his blood pressure soared. He dreaded going into his office every morning because he knew he would waste time weeding through the previous day's mess to get to that day's work. His office caused him so much distress he would often have a headache by noon. Save yourself that anxiety by taking a few minutes to clean up.

> **Take time to plan.**

The old saying goes, "It takes money to make money." The same applies to planning. It takes time to plan, but in the long run it saves time. When you don't plan, you use time inefficiently and leave yourself open to mistakes.

Some people like the rush of adrenaline they get when they leave projects until the last minute. What they don't realize is that eventually they increase their stress level while decreasing their professionalism.

Pam, a communications specialist, felt that she worked best under pressure, so she customarily would stay up all night to finish her projects in a burst of energy. She wrote detailed proposals filled with all of the information a company would need to know about her and her company. Even though she was well qualified, she was losing every consulting bid she submitted. One day she reviewed a few of her proposals, and found dozens of typographical errors. In rushing to complete her proposals, she was compromising the quality of her presentations. Pam started using the spell check on her computer and allowing time to proofread her proposals. She was hired for two consulting jobs soon after that.

Failure to plan ahead can also cost you money. For example, rushing things into overnight express costs a lot more than sending them by first-class mail. When you scramble to get things done, your stress level increases and complications tend to snowball. With a plan to follow, you're less likely to run into last-minute crises.

Practice what I call "selective neglect." That's when you look at your To-Do list, realize that you can't do everything, and choose to neglect those tasks that are not important. Go to the point of completely taking them off your list.

Make it easy to start where you left off. Before you stop working on a project for the day, go one more step and bring it to a point that will make it easy for you to pick it up and finish it at a later date. Projects take longer to finish when you have to play catch-up every time you start working on them.

Follow what I call *structured flexibility*. Structured flexibility is making up your To-Do list and setting your priorities—yet remaining aware your priorities may change at any moment. Even the best plans change. Be willing to change your priorities throughout the day, then refocus on the high-priority tasks.

QUICK TIP FOR HOME OFFICE PROFESSIONALS

Confirm appointments the day before. Sometime before the next day's appointments, call to confirm each one. Sometimes people forget about appointments or wait until the day of the appointment to reschedule. Missed appointments are big time wasters, particularly if you travel to someone's office only to discover that he or she isn't there.

Habits that will make you more productive

Keep the advantages of working at home from becoming disadvantages by developing habits that will make you more productive.

- Make your environment conducive to working. Choose an office space you enjoy, and have your office set up so that when you walk in, you can get to work.

- Set regular office hours. While you don't have to follow the same rigid schedule you may have had in the corporate world, it's a good idea to set hours for yourself. Otherwise it may be noon until you make your first phone call or answer early morning e-mails. Your schedule needs to be flexible, but one that you can follow on a regular basis.

- "Go to work" every day. When you go into your office, treat it as you would an office away from your home. It definitely takes self-discipline to work out of your home, but the benefits make the process worthwhile.

Three types of time

I divide time into the following three types:

1) *Manageable time* is when you don't have any appointments scheduled. You have the day open to use as you please. You can be flexible and productive during this time.

2) *Partially manageable time* is when you are faced with situations that take you away from your work. These situations include interruptions, doctors' appointments, and changes in your schedule that are caused by others, such as someone dropping by your house unexpectedly or a long-distance phone call from someone you haven't talked to in years. Unless you take drastic measures, there isn't much you can do to control what you accomplish during partially manageable time.

3) *Unmanageable time* is when you have specific commitments or appointments. You have to do something or be somewhere at a specific time. This is time that is already scheduled. You have no flexibility about how you use unmanageable time.

During all of these types of time, you will face interruptions, or time-stealers. Knowing how to handle time-stealers will determine how much you accomplish each day. Time-stealers include the following:

- Incoming phone calls
- Uninvited visitors or salespeople
- Looking for lost items
- Distractions
- Equipment breakdowns
- Mail delivery
- Children
- Pets

To find out the particular vulnerablity of time-stealers, fill out the chart on page 223. Track the time-stealers you experience for a week. Once you've recognized the types of interruptions you face, you can start to work on possible ways of dealing with them.

Although some time-stealers are caused by other people, many are self-generated. If your workspace is cluttered, you are more likely to become distracted, which leads to taking attention away from your work or to lose track of items you need, which leads to spending time searching. If you have poor work habits— meaning you procrastinate and don't plan well—you'll end up rushing to meet deadlines, which leads to mistakes and more time lost. If you are unable to say no to people who are imposing on your work time, you may find yourself going from interruption to interruption all day.

TIME STEALERS CHART

Type	Caused By Me	Caused By Others	Solution

©Lisa Kanarek, HomeOfficeLife.com

Handling interruptions

There's little you can do about important meetings, urgent deadlines, or phone calls from clients. These are a part of your work life you have to accommodate each day. Learning to handle the other types of time stealers, however, will make you a much more productive home office professional.

Phone Calls

There must be a law that states that when you are busiest, the phone will ring. Do you ever notice that whenever you need to get work done, the phone rings continuously? On a day when you're not so busy, you may pick up the phone a few times to make sure it still works. To control phone interruptions, I suggest that you do the following:

- *Let your voice mail or answering machine take your calls.* Many people find it difficult to ignore a ringing phone. When you have a deadline to meet, though, you can't afford to answer every call. Turn up the volume on your answering machine or add Caller ID so that you can screen calls as you work. You can always pick up the phone if the call is important.

- *Try to avoid playing telephone tag.* When you leave a message for someone, give a specific time when you will be available to take their return call. When you record your own greeting, ask that the caller indicate the best time for you to return his or her call and give your e-mail or website address in case someone wants to correspond with you immediately or needs information right away.

- *Learn how to get off the phone.* When you've finished talking and have the information you need, wind it down. If someone insists on talking, ask when you can call back.

- *Consider hiring an answering service.* If you hire an answering service to take your calls, you can forward your incoming calls to the service, which frees up your line for outgoing calls. After you get your messages, you can return calls at your convenience. Also, a service makes it look as if you have an assistant. The way a service answers the phone usually sounds as if your personal assistant is taking the call. (See Chapter 13 for more information on phone options.) The disadvantages of a service are that callers may get frustrated because your service can't answer their questions, or they may want to leave a long message or a message in their own words.

- *Take personal calls after hours.* Many people have trouble understanding the idea that home office professionals really are working during the day. You may have to inform your friends that you will not be able to take their calls during the day unless there is an emergency. Make arrangements to call them back after hours at a designated time.

People at Your Door

Until you work at home, it's difficult to imagine what goes on while you're away. Eventually, you'll start noticing who is home all day. If you have neighbors who like to come over to chat, make it clear that you need to work during the day. Friends and family may need gentle reminders that even though you're working at home, you are still running a business.

Ellen, an architect, was tired of commuting and decided to make the move to a home office. Her initial excitement about working at home turned to frustration when her family, who lived nearby, started dropping by for visits. They also started to take advantage of her flexible schedule, calling her to run errands for them. Finally, Ellen discussed the situation with her family and set ground rules. Now they know that her office hours are from 8:30 a.m. to 5:00 p.m., and that she is not available unless there is an emergency.

Children

> An advantage of working at home is that you get to be near your children.

You need to place limitations on how much time you can spend with your children. When you first start to work at home, your children may not understand that even though you're home, you won't be able to spend every minute with them. Although it's challenging, it is possible to have children and operate a business from home.

- Expectant parents who plan to work at home after their baby arrives often figure that babies sleep all the time and therefore they will have a lot of time to work. There's no guarantee that you will get a baby who sleeps often, but even if you do, know that there will be many demands on your time while your child is sleeping. Moreover, if your child must sleep (or occupy himself or herself) every time you have to work, you add tremendous stress to your relationship with your child.

- Recognize from the start that if you are serious about your business, you will need some type of child care. There are many child care options to investigate, from family day care

> You can't (and shouldn't) count on television or naptime to keep your child happily occupied while you work or place business phone calls.

  (your child goes to someone else's house) to at-home child care (a babysitter comes to your home) to a babysitting co-op (you and other parents get together and take turns watching the kids).

- If your child is of preschool age, take him or her to school in the mornings so that you have quiet time to catch up on work. Don't feel guilty that your child isn't home with you at all times. He or she needs to interact with other children.

- For those moments when your child must be with you as you take a business call, keep a box of toys nearby to distract him or her. I recommend, however, that you avoid making business calls with infants and toddlers in the room unless you know your client will understand if they hear a sudden outburst.

- Set up a little table and chair in your office for your child to use. Give him or her a smaller version of a telephone, stapler, tape dispenser, ruler, and safety scissors. Add plenty of paper and markers. Your child will be happy to be in the same room with you, and you'll reduce the number of items being taken out of your desk because your child will have supplies of his or her own. To protect your carpet, place a hard plastic chair mat under your child's work area.

- If your child is old enough, involve him or her in your business. He or she could help you stuff envelopes or put labels on envelopes.

Pets

Pets can be a wonderful addition to a home office and can provide company during the day if you work alone. If you take the time to plan ahead, your pet will be more of an asset than a liability.

- If you have a dog that barks frequently, keep it out of your office during work hours or at least while making phone calls. It's definitely embarrassing to be on the phone when your dog sees another dog and starts barking.

- If you have a pet that sheds, take the time to vacuum or sweep your office often. Otherwise, you run the risk of getting pet hairs in your computer, which could damage it, or on your visitors.

- Make sure your pet has plenty of toys to chew on. I learned the hard way, after my dog chewed one of my CDs.

- Consider getting a second pet to play with the first. If you're out of your office or need to concentrate on a project, you'll face fewer interruptions because your pets will keep each other occupied.

Taking breaks

Working by yourself is so demanding that sometimes the thought of taking half an hour for lunch seems impossible. When you work for someone else, there's always somebody around to "hold the fort," and personal phone calls are often a welcome break throughout the day. None of that applies when you work in a home office.

It's important to take time off for lunch, even if you don't eat much. Think in terms of a car. If you keep driving without stopping for fuel, eventually you're going to run out of gas. Take the time to refuel before you run out of energy.

I recommend to my clients who spend hours working at a computer that they stop working throughout the day and give their eyes and brain a rest.

I also recommend taking walks. By physically getting away from your office, you may mentally be able to take a break. Read your favorite magazine for thirty minutes. Set a timer if you need to.

It's so easy to get involved in what you're doing that you forget to take breaks. Taking breaks throughout the day, however, will actually make you more productive.

Balancing your work life and home life

When you work at home, you are faced with having to mentally switch from work mode to family mode within minutes. You need to strike a balance between your professional and personal lives, even though they happen in the same place. Here are ten ways to find that balance.

1) **Minimize distractions**. Some people say, "I could never work out of my home because I would have too many distractions." As a rule, reduce trips to the kitchen to get something to eat (except at mealtimes), don't turn on the television, and don't let yourself get sidetracked by personal activities such as cleaning the house or doing laundry.

2) **Know when to stop working**. A good friend once told me that she could never have a home office because she wouldn't be able to stop working. When you work at home, you don't have far to go when you get the urge to get one more project finished. If you're single, it probably doesn't matter how long you work, but if you have a family, you will soon hear complaints from all sides. When you stop working, really stop. Close the door to your office or close up your desk and concentrate on your family.

3) **Don't eat lunch at your desk**. When you take a lunch break, leave your office and eat in another part of your home. Changing your scenery and physically removing yourself from your work will help to clear your mind.

4) **Schedule regular "dates" with your spouse and children**. A freelance artist I know blocks out every

Wednesday afternoon to spend with her husband. They play golf or tennis or go out to lunch. They both know that every Wednesday afternoon is their time to play, no matter what else is going on during the rest of the week.

5) **Take at least one weekday off per month to play**. At the beginning of each month, schedule a day when you are going to stay completely out of your office and do something else. This would be an ideal day to catch up on reading, see a movie you've been wanting to see, or just enjoy the outdoors. Let your voice mail take your calls. You'll find that taking a day off will prepare you for a month of productive work.

6) **Make a list of fun things you've always wanted to do, then start doing them**. Maybe you've always wanted to visit the local art museum but never seemed to have the time. Start checking your local newspapers for activities and upcoming attractions. If you have lived in the same city for years, consider taking a guided tour of the city. You'll learn more about your city in a few hours than you had in several years. The point is to keep your horizons open and not let your work consume your life. The activities you engage in will inform your work and enliven your outlook.

7) **Use your office for business-related activities only**. Rather than go to your office to read your favorite magazine or new mystery, go somewhere else in your home. This will keep you in the mindset that your office is for business and the rest of your home is for your personal life.

8) **Don't use other parts of your home for business on a regular basis**. If you have a favorite chair where you sit and read or watch television, don't use it for work. After awhile, it will no longer be a place for you to relax and get away.

9) **Include your spouse in your business**. Even though you may work in unrelated fields, it's always good to get an outside point of view. Your spouse may be able to give you a solution to a problem you've had on your mind for days. The most obvious answer is sometimes not seen by the person closest to the problem. Also, if your spouse understands your work

and what it involves, he or she will be less likely to resent all of the hours you put into it.

10) **If you and your spouse work together, avoid talking about business after hours**. I know many successful business partners who are also married. They tell me that one of the keys to making this arrangement work is to get away from work for a while and relax. When you're finished working for the day, talk about something other than work.

A word about vacations. If you ever worked for someone else, one week may not have seemed long enough for a vacation. Now that you work for

> It's important to recharge your batteries by taking time off.

yourself, taking one week off may seem unthinkable. Do it anyway. At the beginning of each year, block out one week segments (at least twice) when you will go on vacation and treat that time as sacred. Don't schedule appointments during that time, and don't bring work with you if you go away.

Time is a valuable resource of which we may never feel we get enough. Technology, however, is working to change all that. There are devices that promise to give us more time, make our lives easier, and put us ahead of everyone else. In the next chapter, you'll see that by means of the latest electronic equipment, the average home office on Main Street can now keep up with an office on Wall Street.

The Electronic
Home Office

The Electronic Home Office

Technology changes daily. What may be state-of-the-art today may be obsolete in six months. With this in mind, I've written this chapter as a guide to finding the right technology to suit your needs. Realize, however, that as you read this, something new, better, and faster is just around the corner.

> The right equipment can enhance your productivity, improve your professionalism and increase your bottom line.

Telephones—making the right connection

The first piece of equipment you need is a telephone. Your phone is your link to the outside world, and it affects how you make a first impression. If you have a phone that sounds as if you're talking into a tin can, the impression you make is an unprofessional one.

Features to look for when purchasing a phone

- A *hold button* is more effective and more professional than covering the receiver and hoping the person on the other end can't hear you.

- A *mute button* works well in case you have to cough, respond to someone else in the room, or quiet a barking dog without disrupting your conversation. You can still hear your caller, but he or she can't hear noises on your end.

- *Automatic redial* saves time dialing numbers that are busy.

- *Number storage* is used to recall those numbers you dial frequently.

- *Multiline capacity* will help you meet your growing office needs. Think ahead—this is a convenience you may not need now, but will appreciate in the future.

- A *speaker phone* allows you to dial without holding the receiver. While you're waiting for an answer, you can keep working. Use the speaker feature only until you get an answer, because it's rude to place someone on the speaker phone when you're talking. Another option is to use a cordless headset (see next section).

- *Cordless phone*s give you freedom to walk around your office—or even outside. I know someone who would take his portable phone to the pool in the summer and make his calls from there.

Telephone headsets

If you want to minimize background noise or keep your hands free while you make and take calls, use a headset.

- Cordless headsets keep both hands free and eliminate the need for a cord. Plus they give you the freedom to walk around your office or house. (One of my clients makes most of his calls poolside.)

- Most headsets resemble a headband, yet are not cumbersome.

- Some headphones allow you to replace your phone with a phone/keyboard combo that plugs into your keyboard port and lets you make calls from your computer.

How many lines do you need?

You should have separate personal and business lines. You may even want more than one business line. Whether or not you want to pay the cost of installing an additional business line depends on how many calls you currently receive or projects you will receive, as well as the number of outbound calls you make. If you make calls all day, I recommend two business lines in your office, one for incoming and the other for outgoing.

Consider other equipment in your office with regard to phone lines. If you still have a dial-up connection, you will need at least two phone lines—one to make and receive business calls, and the other so that you can be online at the same time.

If you receive several faxes every day, and use your modem throughout the day, install a separate fax/modem line to keep you business line free. If you have an Internet connection other than dial-up and receive only a few faxes per week, one business line should be sufficient.

> It's a good idea, yet not absolutely necessary, to have your fax machine on a separate line.

When you first open a home office, you may not want to spend the extra money to get a separate business line. However, you probably don't want to keep using your personal line as your business number. In some states it is illegal to do so and could result in a fine. If you add a business line, you'll be listed in directory assistance and in the white and yellow pages of the phone book, which will make it easier for people to find you. If you write an article or receive publicity and no one is able to contact you, the publicity will be of no value to your business.

Arlene, a video consultant, works with people throughout the country. She didn't want to incur the expense of installing a business line, but after several clients told her how difficult it had been to locate her, she finally relented. The money she was saving by not having a separate business line was outweighed by the business she was losing.

Another factor to keep in mind is taxes. If you use your personal line for business, you won't be able to deduct those expenses at the end of the year.

Note: Some home office professionals are replacing their business lines with a cellular phone, especially those who are rarely in their home offices.

Phone services

Services available from the phone company vary from state to state. Sometimes phone companies will offer specials wherein they will initiate new services for free. At other times, they may charge a start-up fee. Check with your local phone company to see what is available to you and at what cost. Of the many features available, here are a few:

- *Call waiting.* If you're on the phone and someone else is trying to call you at the same time, call waiting will interrupt you with a beep to let you know you have another call. This is nice because you never need to miss an important call, and it's nice for your clients because they hear a ring instead of a busy signal. The downside of call waiting is that interrupting your phone conversation can be awkward, although you always have the option of ignoring the other call or disabling call waiting by pressing *70. A more professional alternative to Call Waiting is Call Notes.

- *Call Notes.* If you are already on the phone when someone calls in, the call will automatically switch to your voice mail. You could leave a message explaining that you're currently on the phone and will return the call if the caller leaves a name and number. With this voice mail system, you can also give the caller several options. For example, if he pressed 1, he could hear information about your services; if he pressed 2, he could receive information from you, and if he pressed 3, he could leave a message. Voice mail may be a service offered by your phone company, and voice-mail boards can be purchased to add onto your computer.

- *Caller ID.* With Caller ID, you can screen your calls while you're working on important projects, know who called while you were out (complete with phone numbers in most cases) and avoid annoying sales calls.

- *Call forwarding.* This feature allows you to forward all of the calls that come to your phone number to another number. You can forward your business calls to your personal line or wireless phone.

- *Three-way calling.* This feature allows you to talk with more than one person at a time. It's especially helpful in setting up conference calls so that your home location is not a liability.

- *Tele-branching, or remote call forwarding.* This feature allows you to "keep" your phone number if you move. Callers who dial your old number will reach you at your new number.

- *Auto redial.* If you've tried to reach someone and keep getting a busy signal, auto redial will continue to call until the other person's line is free. When the call is completed, your phone will ring. When you pick up your phone, you'll hear the other person's phone ringing.

- *Distinctive Ringing.* This feature assigns various numbers (all on one line) special ringing patterns. For example, you could assign your fax number a special ring and only answer the phone after a standard ring. These patterns let you know on which number someone is trying to call you.

Electronic answering systems

The way you handle your incoming phone calls can mean the difference between landing a big deal and seeing that deal slip through your fingers. The rapidly changing world of messaging technology offers several options for handling calls and helping reduce the amount of time between receiving a message and returning the call.

You can use a simple voice mail system available from your local phone company or other provider; integrate your computer and telephone into a screening, answering and messaging system—or utilize a service that offers an electronic assistant available 24 hours a day, 7 days a week. There are, of course, two non-technical solutions—an answering service, which can be expensive and at times unresponsive and unprofessional, or a full-time receptionist (who requires insurance benefits and vacation time).

A voice mail system may be adequate for a small business that handles relatively few calls each day (less than 15). A few time-saving features include the ability to revise your outgoing message quickly; the capability to link your system with a pager, thus reducing the time between a call and call-back; and a popular feature that routes a caller to your outgoing message if you are on the phone (a better option than a busy signal or call waiting).

If you receive more than 30 calls a day, or more than you can handle, a program installed within your computer may give you the extra help you need. You can screen your calls, look up numbers quickly and add your pager into the mix to become even more accessible to your clients. A major drawback may be the logistics of owning a second computer and adding a phone line dedicated to handling your incoming calls.

A multi-task system works in conjunction with your computer. These products offer various functions including an automatic attendant, pager notification, fax tone detection, fax-on-demand capabilities, voice mail and background operation so you can still run programs while the system is taking calls.

If missing one phone call could be detrimental to your business, if you need to be readily accessible to your clients, and if want to go beyond using a pager, an electronic assistant may be your best option. There are various fully automated, voice-activated communications tools available through service providers. These systems utilize the latest voice digitization and recognition technology. They maintain a complete list of your clients, so if you want to call a particular client, you merely say the system's name and say, "Call Mary Smith," and the service does the rest. If you have to be out of your office for a period of time, the system makes sure that your clients can reach you after you tell it whether you'll be in your car, home, or other location—or it will take messages for you.

Tips for making the most of voice mail

There are several ways to make your voice mail more effective:

- When recording your message, remember to let the caller know within the first few seconds how he or she can bypass your message.

- Keep your outgoing message short and simple and vary it often. Always include your name and company, ask for a detailed message and make sure your voice sounds clear. Consider adding your e-mail or website address to your message.

- When recording your message, let the caller know if he or she has a limited amount of time to leave a message and ask the caller for the best time to return their call. You'll save hours of phone tag by knowing when someone will be in his or her office to take your return call. When you leave messages, do the same.

- Don't save all of your voice messages. Instead, take action. After writing down or entering the message and number, erase the voice mail message.

How to be more effective on the phone

Some people consider the telephone just another piece of home office equipment, much as they would a fax or computer. Others view it as more. They see it not as a phone line but a gold mine. They realize that it's not the equipment that makes their business profitable, instead it's how they use it—and they use it to make a fortune. You can make the time you spend on the phone more profitable by taking a close look at how you use your phone.

- *Make calls on optimal days and during the best times.* Some people are morning people while others wait until late afternoon to function at their maximum capacity. Monday morning is usually not a good time to call someone for the first time. That is when people organize their week, recover from the weekend or attend meetings. On Tuesday and Wednesday, the week is already underway and they will be more receptive to your call.

> As they say, timing is everything. Do everything you can to call at the right time.

- *Know what you're going to say ahead of time.* Highlight the key points you want to convey while speaking with a client. In case your mind wanders, you'll be able to pick up where you left off.

- *Make phone appointments.* When someone asks you to call them back, schedule a mutually beneficial time to call. By doing so, you will ensure that they are there when you call. Send in advance any information that you will discuss in the call (if necessary) and call at the agreed upon time. Treat phone calls the same way as face-to-face appointments and keep them.

- *List all of the calls you need to make, and call during one time period.* When you make a commitment to send something, add it to your To-Do list and follow up in the afternoon. Stopping after each call to compile the information you promised or fulfill the commitments you made, could affect the rest of your calls. When you are in a "calling mode," you will accomplish more. Especially since it may take a few calls to get "warmed up."

- *Keep detailed notes when talking with clients.* Rather than take notes on loose scraps of paper, use a contact management software program, your PDA, sheets within a daily planner, a spiral notebook or papers kept in client files. You will save time searching for client notes if you keep them in one place.

- *Be courteous to anyone who answers the phone.* When calling someone, you may think that you are talking to the receptionist, when in fact you are speaking with the president of the company. Many deals have been squelched because of a misunderstanding as simple as that. Oftentimes you may be dealing with egos as fragile as a piece of fine china. One false move and the entire deal may be shattered.

- *Have a standard method for getting rid of long-winded callers.* There are some people who will call you, tell you what they need and hang up. There are others who seem to have endless hours to talk—and do—if you let them. When you're surrounded by work, deadlines and commitments, be aggressive. Tell the person that you have a meeting, have to take another call or the truth, you have no time to talk. Make arrangements to call them later or in the evening.

Keeping track of phone messages

If you're the only one answering your phone or taking messages from your voice mail, you don't have to worry about phone message slips. Use either a telephone log, contact management program or a plain spiral notebook to keep track of messages. Enter the date, time, caller's name, company, and message.

When you use a phone log, notebook or computer program, you cut down on the number of scraps of paper in your office, and you have a convenient way of looking up clients' phone numbers. With a running record of both incoming and outgoing calls, you can easily track your long distance calls and calls that should be billed to clients.

If you advertise in various publications or through other media, manually or electronically track the phone calls you receive as a result to see how effective your ads are. This will help you decide whether or not to renew these ads.

You'll also want to keep track of referrals. If a caller was referred by someone, make a note of that person's name so that you can send a thank-you note. Although technology prevails, a hand-written note is still a nice touch.

PHONE LOG				
DATE	NAME	COMPANY	NUMBER	MESSAGE

A phone log like this one helps you keep track of your work-related calls.
©Lisa Kanarek, HomeOfficeLife.com

Buying the right computer

The home office of today needs at least one computer to keep up with all of today's business needs. You cannot be competitive, regardless of your business, without a computer.

> Computers have proven to be invaluable to the home office professional.

When Michelle worked in a corporate office, she never learned how to use a computer because her administrative assistant did all of her typing for her. When she opened her home office, she felt she was computer illiterate but didn't want to spend endless hours learning how to use a computer. She also believed that she could do whatever she needed to do without a computer.

Michelle's spouse convinced her that a computer would make her life easier. After he detailed the various ways she could use a computer in her work—and because she was a wedding planner, there were plenty—she was convinced that a computer would help her. She feared, however, that learning to use a computer would be too difficult. After she bought a computer, she hired an in-home consultant to show her the basics and her business has grown ever since.

Some people are avid Apple Macintosh (Mac) supporters, whereas others would never consider replacing their Windows® operated computers. There used to be vast differences between Macintosh and Windows® computers—one being that Macs were easier to maneuver and Windows® computers cheaper. Macs are now priced competitively with Windows® computers. Further, with the introduction of platform-crossing programs the gap between the two has narrowed.

Also, most widely-used programs are now available for both platforms, meaning you can use the same file types on either type of computer. The platform choice may now be based on your personal preference.

If you already own a computer and want to upgrade, you'll know what you want your new computer to do. If you've never had a computer, consider these questions before you make the investment.

- *Why are you buying the computer?* Do you need to do word processing, desktop publishing, software development, graphics, or bookkeeping? Find software that suits your needs—and then buy a computer that is compatible with the software.

- *How much are you willing to spend?* Remember that this is an investment in your business.

- *Will you be able to upgrade your system as your business grows?* In time, you may need more sophisticated computer capabilities. The bottom line is does it have enough memory? Buy more than you need. You'll need it eventually.

- *What type of support is available if something goes wrong with it?* Make sure you buy from a reputable source.

- *How long is the warranty?* Will you have any trouble getting your computer serviced?

- *Do you want a desktop system or laptop?* Many people want both, yet can't afford two systems. If money is an issue, yet you're on the road most of the time, opt for a laptop system and use it in your office as well. You can attach a full-size monitor to your laptop while in your office.

- *Will you know how to use it?* If not, will you be able to get technical support in a timely manner?

Computer maintenance

Use a surge protector at all times for all of your equipment. To protect your investment even further, unplug everything in your office, including your computer, during a lightning storm. A surge protector cannot stop a "direct hit" from lightning. Some surge protector manufacturers have "insurance for losses" due to a surge, a lifetime product warranty, and Internet connection protection. If you have a modem, unplug your computer and phone to avoid blowing integrated circuits.

Add additional protection against a data loss during a power outage by investing in a reliable alternate power supply (its primary purpose is to keep you running—not protection against surges). You won't lose data or downtime through power surges, and in the event of an extended power failure you'll have ample time to save files and shut down safely.

You may install a "screen saver" program for security and entertainment value (Screen savers used to be used to avoid burning an image into old monochrome monitors, but are no longer needed for that reason.) A screen saver equipped with a feature that requires a password to reactivate will protect your computer from kids and spouses if you leave your office for a while.

Protect your computer from dust by using a soft nylon dust cover. Protect it from viruses on the inside by installing antivirus programs.

Make sure your office has enough power to handle your office equipment. Otherwise, you may constantly blow fuses or cause power surges.

Choosing the right printer

Which computer you choose is your first decision, but because you're in a home office, it's not what your clients will see first. What they'll see is the output from your computer. When shopping for a printer, consider the following factors:

- *Is it compatible with your computer?*

- *What is the quality of the printing?* Laser printers give the highest quality printing. The print from dot matrix printers ranges in quality from acceptable to excellent.

- *Does it print in color?* This feature is becoming standard in many businesses. Consider adding a color ink jet or color laser printer to spice up your marketing and sales materials and use it along with your black and white printer.

- *What is the paper capacity?* The more paper a printer holds, the less time you'll spend having to add more.

- *Does it have a straight-through paper feed, or does the paper go from the top to the bottom of the printer, causing it to curl?*

- *How many pages per minute does it print?*

- *Look at the "footprint," or the amount of desktop space it needs, including the paper tray.* Can you accommodate it?

- *Is it affordable?* It should be since printer costs have dropped considerably.

- *Is it network compatible?* (You may eventually put a mini-network in your home if you haven't already done so.)

Monitor

A larger screen and a quality anti-glare screen will reduce eyestrain. If you suffer from neck problems, use a special desk that allows you to place your monitor at desk level under a viewing screen.

Another, appealing option (yet more expensive) is a slim LCD panel. Some panels, a light as six pounds and only a half-inch thick, provide quality resolution and occupy minimal space. A few features of LCD panels include a power save mode that detects when you've walked away from your computer. One second after it senses your return, it automatically returns to active mode. Another feature allows the panel to automatically adjust to the appropriate monitor brightness according to the level of ambient light in your office.

CD-ROM drive

You'll need either an internal or external CD drive to read Compact Disks. If you're installing software, you'll need a CD drive. A CD-RW (writer/rewriter) is a more efficient way to save data than on a removable disk or Zip. It may take more time unless you have a fast burner.

Computer programs

The number of computer programs available to help you organize your day, projects, and finances can be staggering. A quick check of computer user groups, online special interest areas, or computer-oriented publications can save you time and money and help you avoid buying programs that won't meet your needs.

Different people need different programs, so for me to tell you which programs to use would be presumptuous. Determine what you want a program to do, then find the right software to satisfy your needs.

> Many programs offer downloadable versions so you can try a program before you buy it.

Organizing your data

A computer is a great organizing tool, but it creates some organizational challenges.

- Use a holder to store your disks (floppy, Zip, and CDs). Holders come in a wide variety of sizes and styles. Keep the disks and CDs you use more often within reach.

- Label your disks clearly. Write the name of the general categories of documents on the label so that you won't have to open each document to find out what is on the disk. There are computer programs that keep a catalog of files on removable media so you can readily retrieve the documents you need from the right disk. These programs are relatively inexpensive. As your file storage needs increase, so does your need for these types of programs.

- At the end of each day, back up any updated or new information on your hard drive that you consider important and not easily replaced. Regularly perform full system backups. The method of backup depends upon the volume of data and the amount of money and time you are willing to invest.

- When you're working on a long document, back it up every ten to fifteen minutes. Otherwise, if you have a system error or power failure, you could lose everything. Some programs have a backup system built in. There are also utility programs that have this function.

- Go through your hard drive once a month and purge the documents you no longer need. File management software makes file purging easier. If you generate large numbers of files or multiple drafts of documents, these programs are a necessity and time-saver.

- Give your computer files the same names as the files in your file cabinet. If you have a hanging folder labeled *Correspondence* in your file cabinet, label the directory *Correspondence*, too.

- Keep the same type of computer information together. For example, all sales letters should be together and all client information should be with other information pertaining to your clients.

- Protect disk or tape backups by storing them in a fireproof safe or off-site.

- Keep your documents separate from your applications and create document files organized by category (i.e. correspondence, marketing projects, ideas, etc.). Make two backups of any important information.

- Another option is to create aliases for documents that allow you to keep one copy of the document with an application and another in a working file. (This applies to Macintosh and Windows users.)

Backup systems

One of the best investments you can make is in a reliable backup system. You can choose between removable media drives, external hard drives or additional drives (some computers come with two hard drives). Test your backup system periodically to make sure that your information has been saved properly.

> Hardware is easy (albeit costly) to replace, while some data is irreplaceable.

Each of the following backup options is add-on equipment for many computers. Your choice depends on how much data you want to store and how much money you want to spend. There are a variety of storage options, ranging from floppy disks to magneto-optical and writable CDs. Some methods are being supplanted by other technologies, but all offer reliable service. Base your choice on your needs and your budget. I recommend you choose one and use it.

Data tapes

They are cheap and reliable and are used for backup instead of working documents. They are used less frequently since you can't work directly from them.

High capacity storage

Some people refer to these as "disks on steroids." This removable media, such as the Zip, Jazz, or EZ Flyer, offers cheap, reliable types of backup. They are almost the same size as 3.5" disks—only thicker and may hold up to 2 GB of data. High-density removable media is reliable, readily portable and saves space in your office. These disks are also good for moving data back and forth between computers and allow you to use these files in another machine, if necessary, if you have a portable drive. Other similar systems such as miniature hard drives, memory keys, etc. are being introduced now and will be more common.

External hard drive

One factor to consider when purchasing an external hard drive is comparing reliability and speed (access and data transfer). You can set up and use an external hard drive to boot and run your machine in case your internal disk crashes. Very fast, very large capacity disks are readily available and are increasingly affordable.

Laptop (portable) computers

If you're on the road more than you are in your home office, a laptop computer will give you access to the information you need when you need it. Most home office professionals don't have an assistant in the office who can give them the information they need, so a laptop computer is appealing.

- *Laptops operate on battery or AC current.* They will generally fit inside a briefcase and weigh under 6 pounds.

- *PDAs*, small hand-held computers.

What to look for when buying a portable computer

Use the following guidelines for buying a portable:

- Consider the size and weight. If you're going to take it with you when you travel, will you have the room for it and will it be light enough to take with you?

- Make sure that the battery life is long enough for you.

- Check to make sure the resolution of the display can accommodate the software or applications you plan to use.

- Test the keyboard to make sure your fingers are not cramped.

- Is the processor fast enough?

- Make sure the portable has enough memory for your needs.

- Does the portable have peripheral capabilities? You may want the option of connecting a modem, printer, scanner, or fax machine.

- Invest in security software since many laptops are stolen. You don't want critical information to fall into the wrong hands.

Modems

There are internal and external modems. The technology for modems is changing so rapidly that I suggest you invest in an external modem for now. Also, with DSL, cable, and other Internet connection alternatives, modems will one day become obsolete. Before you buy a modem, consider these suggestions:

- Buy the highest speed possible and make sure the modem is compatible with your computer.

- If you are going to use your modem throughout the day, use a line separate from your business line to keep your business line open to receive calls.

- If you're on the road often, use an external modem while away and use the same modem when you return to your office.

Facts on faxes

We used to depend upon the postal service to deliver our mail. Then there was the option of overnight or even same-day delivery, followed by the fax machine which gives us the ability to transfer documents anywhere in minutes. (Now the fax faces stiff competition from Internet communication alternatives.)

If you are spending a fortune on faxes (as much as $4 per outgoing page and $2 for incoming), and wasting time driving somewhere to send and receive faxes, invest in a fax machine. Your options are a fax modem or a stand-alone fax machine.

Fax modems

Some people are eager to get rid of external equipment and are happy to receive and send faxes from their computer, while others don't want to worry about receiving faxes within their computer, then printing them. With a fax modem, if you have to fax a paper-based document, you'll have to scan it into your computer before faxing it. Also, fax modems are not always able to communicate with older fax machines.

Plain-paper machines

The ideal fax machine is a plain-paper one (thermal copies eventually fade) because of the copy quality and the added feature of a copy machine.

Fax tips

Use the following guidelines to get the most out of your fax machine:

- Set up a fax area complete with cover sheets, pens and extra rolls of fax paper or sheets for your fax.

- On your cover sheet, list what you are faxing to ensure that the other party receives everything you've faxed. Remember to have your business name, address, telephone number, fax number and e-mail address on the cover sheet. An alternative to a full-size cover sheet is small, self-adhesive fax notes. By attaching one of these notes to your document, you'll save money on airtime, as well as paper on the other end.

- A note about fax etiquette: Don't transmit faxes in the middle of the night to someone you know has a home office. Instead, send all faxes during the day or early evening. Otherwise, you risk awakening the recipient's family and you'll undoubtedly annoy that person. If you were attempting to sell them something, don't count on making the sale.

- Don't send unsolicited faxes. If the recipient is not interested in your service, you'll waste their fax paper and if they ever need to use your service, they will no longer have the fax anyway.

- Don't send reams of faxes that aren't immediate and could be sent by e-mail, overnight mail or US. mail instead.

- Before you send a fax, if you have call waiting, disable it by pushing *70 on your phone. Otherwise you run the risk of disconnecting while faxing. In general, if you send and receive several faxes each day, find an alternative to call waiting to ensure your faxes arrive without any problems.

- If you're working in a home office and you're tired of hearing a loud fax tone when you answer your phone, consider adding Distinct Ring to your phone service. With Distinct Ring you can give clients a second number that you use for faxes. When someone calls your fax number, you will hear a series of short, double rings. If you hear a regular ring, you know it's your business line. Of course, if you receive many faxes each day, dedicate another line to your fax machine to avoid tying up your business line.

- If you are transmitting a fax to someone in a large corporation, let the person know ahead of time in case the fax machine is located several floors away. Otherwise, call the person after you've transmitted the information to make sure he or she received your fax.

- Make sure your fax has enough memory to store at least ten pages in case your machine runs out of paper when you're away from your office.

- Consider using an Internet-based fax service. Some are even free.

Copiers

Investing in a copier can save you innumerable trips to the local copy center. Various copiers are designed for home office use. The following are the features to look for in a copier:

- *Size.* Do you have room to store it? If it has a moving plate (the surface on which you place your originals), make sure there is enough room for it to move back and forth.

- *Quality of copies.* If the copy quality is marginal, you'll still be spending time at the copy center. Paying more does not necessarily guarantee better quality, so test each machine carefully before you buy.

- *Cost of supplies and maintenance.* If the copier is priced low but the toner cartridges are expensive, you will wind up spending more in the long run than you would at a copy center.

- *Copy sizes.* Do you need to reduce or enlarge copies? Do you need legal- and letter-size copies?

- *Paper tray.* If you make only a small number of copies, it may not matter if you have to hand feed each sheet. If you make multiple copies throughout the day, you'll want a copier with a paper tray and automatic feed.

Multifunction peripherals

Multifunction peripherals (MFPs) are adored by some people and despised by others. These machines combine printing, scanning, copying, and faxing functions in one unit. If you compared the cost of buying each piece of equipment separately vs. an all-in-one system, you'd save money on the MFP.

Make sure that you're satisfied with the quality of each function before you invest in an MFP. Also, keep in mind that if one feature no longer works, you'll be without the other features until the machine is fixed. If you want to save space, an MFP may be your best bet.

Video conferencing

The size and cost of videoconferencing equipment continues to shrink. Instead of being limited to voice contact, you can "meet" with a client "face-to-face." If you have a virtual office, with employees spread throughout the country, you can hold regular staff meetings with each person in his or her own home office. Keep in mind that if you make use of this technology, you'll need to "dress the part" when meeting with clients via video. Also, make sure that whatever background your client sees is professional.

The Internet

The Internet is a good way to market your business, obtain research materials quickly and visually communicate with others who are in their own home offices around the world. There are a few ways to save time using the Internet.

- As you discover websites that you know you'll visit again, add them to your bookmark list. Instead of typing in a long address, you simply go to your bookmark list and find the site you need. If you find you're collecting a large number of bookmarks, use a bookmark manager. There are programs that will integrate URLs (website addresses) for ready access, and programs with an "auto-surf" feature that loads pages for you to browse later, thus saving you time.

- Keep a list of your favorite websites in your planner (see Chapter 6).

- Resist the temptation to print or download everything you see. Be selective. Also, make sure that you've installed a reliable virus protector before you download any information.

Connecting to the Internet

If you're looking for speed, ease of connection and a way to avoid being "knocked offline," you have a few options. The main ones are a Digital Subscriber Line (DSL), ISDN (Integrated Services Digital Network), and cable modem. Some satellite systems offer Internet service too.

DSL: Operated by the local phone company, DSL is always on and utilizes standard phone lines.

> Modems and phone lines are no longer the only way to connect to the Internet.

ISDN: It is always on too and utilizes fast data transmission over standard copper phone wires. ISDN lines are fast, but not as fast as cable or DSL.

Cable: It is always on and operates at a fast speed. It is usually priced at a flat rate. It's not available everywhere and traffic on the line can affect speed.

Turning Your Car Into a Functional Office

Turning Your Car Into a Functional Office 14

Today your car can be an extension of your home office. Cell phones, laptops, portable printers, PDAs and other technology make it easy to work anywhere. Some people's cars look like a home and an office combined. They have clothing in the trunk, books and magazines in the back seat, and food up front. It takes more than just bringing technology with you in your car to make it a functional office. You need to set it up logically and without clutter.

You can take it with you

Stephen, a sales rep, never knew what materials his clients would want, so he usually guessed. He would throw some sales sheets in the car before appointments and hope they would be the right ones. If they turned out to be the wrong ones, he would send further information later. Soon he noticed that his postal expenses were getting out of hand, and he realized he was spending a lot of time writing cover letters to accompany the additional information.

We set up files in Stephen's trunk with a few complete sets of all the sales information he had. Each month he would replace the sales materials he had given out. Whenever he found he was missing some paperwork a client wanted, he only had to go out to his car to get it.

It happens to everyone. You go to mail some documents at the post office and you realize you need to include a note, but you don't have any stationery with you. You have to go back to your office, then back to the post office, and by the time your paperwork is mailed you are behind schedule and thoroughly irritated. Solve this problem by creating a car office kit.

QUICK TIP FOR HOME OFFICE PROFESSIONALS

If you're on the road a lot, be good to your car. Get on a regular maintenance schedule, even though trips to the garage are a nuisance. Preventive maintenance will ultimately save you money and possibly the humiliation of missing an important meeting because of a breakdown.

How to create a car office kit

Start with a box with a lid, a soft-sided bag, or a briefcase that will stay in your car at all times. Pick a size that will fit in your trunk, on the back seat, or on the floor of the passenger side of your car. Wherever you keep your kit, make sure it's accessible and that it won't slide around or get in your way. In your car office kit put whatever items you will need, including the following:

- Letterhead, notecards, and envelopes
- A roll of stamps
- Calculator
- Pens/pencils
- Pad of paper
- Paper clips
- Staple remover
- Small stapler
- Small scissors
- Tape dispenser
- Rubber bands
- Napkins (for those unavoidable meals in the car)
- Change for tolls and parking

- Minicassette recorder for taking notes
- A clear, plastic zippered pouch to hold maps and important documents (car registration, insurance card)

Remember to restock your supplies when they run low.

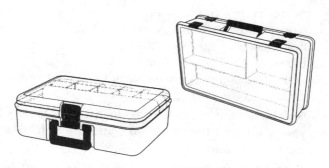

Keep all of your supplies organized in one case. (Courtesy of Iris)

Files—not piles

In your home office, you store papers vertically in files, rather than horizontally in piles. The same principle applies to your car. If you don't store papers properly in your car, there's a good chance you'll lose them or that they'll get ruined. Keep papers and sales literature easily accessible and safe by storing them in files or notebooks. You can't bring your file cabinet into your car, but there are other options that will work.

A portable file box will organize your papers in your car. (Courtesy of Leeco Industries)

A sturdy file box makes it easy to transport files from your office to your car. It holds hanging folders with file folders and will keep your papers stationary. You could also use it to hold catalogs or other sales material that you want to take with you. It is small enough to fit in your trunk or back seat.

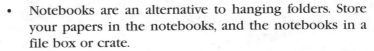

A portable file box is a good way to transport a few file folders. (Courtesy of Eldon)

- "Milk crate" file holders, sturdy and functional, also hold hanging folders with file folders. They're small enough to store on the backseat or in the trunk of your car.

- Notebooks are an alternative to hanging folders. Store your papers in the notebooks, and the notebooks in a file box or crate.

- A portable file holder works well if you don't need to keep many files in your car. Several companies make small file holders that have handles and snap shut. They have room for files inside and room for supplies on top.

Helpful car office organizing products

Most manufacturers have special divisions within the company whose job it is to develop products to make our lives easier. They identify an organizing problem and design the ideal product to solve that problem.

> When you outfit your car office, try thinking like a major manufacturer.

Before you buy any equipment for your car, determine what your challenges are. Then find the product that will help you meet that challenge. The following are a few options:

- A *visor organizer* clips to your visor and holds extra pens, change, and any other small items you need to have readily accessible.

- A *clipboard* is useful when you need a writing surface in your car. You could use a basic clipboard or buy one that has storage room inside.

- A little *note pad with a suction cup* will attach to the inside of your car.

- A *cup holder* will prevent coffee spills on your paperwork.

- A *holder with pockets* that attaches to the back of one of the front seats can be used for all sorts of supplies.

- A *trunk organizer* will store emergency equipment such as tools, flares, and jumper cables, and will keep them from knocking into your office supplies.

- Don't forget a *trash bag* to keep your car from getting cluttered..

Your briefcase—the link between car and home office

Transporting papers back and forth from your home office to your car and from your car to appointments can result in lost papers. A briefcase can solve that problem.

You will save time and be more efficient if you make the effort to organize your briefcase. Even a state-of-the-art briefcase will work only as well as you organize it.

- Use file folders labeled **To Do**, **To File**, **To Read**, and **To Do on Return**. When you get back to your home office, take out all of the folders and sort the papers into their correct places in your home office.

- Before you leave for an appointment, make sure everything you need is in your briefcase. You're more likely to remember all of your important paperwork if you make a note on your To-Do list to pack exactly what you need. You may want to go as far as using a different briefcase for each activity in which you are involved. For example, you could use one case for a division of your company and another for volunteer work.

- The *Sort-Pal* is a favorite among my home office clients because it makes it easy to transport papers from one place to another. It's ideal for holding papers that need to be copied or faxes that need to be sent while you're on the road. It has six dividers with preprinted labels, and also comes with blank labels so that you can customize it.

The Sort-Pal is useful for transporting papers. (Courtesy of Esselte Corporation)

Keeping track of mileage

If you plan to claim mileage on your income tax, you need to keep accurate records. There are a few ways to ensure you'll have the documentation you'll need in the event you are audited:

- Record your business mileage in the travel section of your planning notebook.

- Or, write down your business mileage on the blank page facing your To-Do sheet in your planning notebook or enter the information in your PDA.

- Another option is to keep a steno pad in your glove compartment and use columns to record the date, point of departure, destination, and miles traveled.

Cellular phones

For some, a cellular phone is a luxury, whereas for others it's a necessity. In some professions, being able to respond quickly to a client may mean the difference between making a sale and losing it to a competitor. In other professions, it may mean the difference between life and death.

My father is a pediatrician, and for years the joke in our family was that he knew where every pay phone was in every theater, restaurant, and store in the city. After Dad bought a cell phone, he couldn't believe how much time he used to waste searching for pay phones. When his answering service pages him, he is able to respond quickly and take care of his patients immediately. To determine if you need a cell phone, ask yourself the following questions:

1) If you have a pager, are you constantly searching for the nearest pay phone?

2) Do you spend more than $30 a month on calls from pay phones? (Don't forget to figure in the amount of money you spend on gas driving around trying to find a phone, as well as the amount of time you spend searching.)

3) Are you unable to return all of the calls you receive each day?

4) Are you missing business opportunities because you're unreachable while you're on the road?

5) Do you have clients with strange hours?

6) Are you out of your office more than in it?

7) Do you travel long distances to appointments?

8) Do you need to be more accessible to clients?

If you answered yes to any of the foregoing questions, a cellular phone could be a worthwhile investment for you. They make efficient use of "down time" when you would otherwise just be driving around.

Additions to cellular phones

Cellular phones come in various sizes. Some people prefer a smaller phone while others fear they'll lose anything not as large as a home phone. In addition to the phone itself are other add-ons:

- A phone kit comes with a bracket that you can mount on your dashboard. You can use a speaker mounted near your visor or attach a headset

- A charger that plugs into your lighter is ideal for the times you forget to charge your phone at the end of the day.

- A phone clip that attaches to your belt ensures you don't miss a call, especially if the phone is set on vibrate.

Cellular phones continue to decrease in size and increase in capabilities. They have all of the features available in your home office phone, including call waiting, call forwarding and conference calling. Some even have games to keep you entertained in between appointments, and allow you to send and receive text messages—as well as access the Internet A cellular phone will work for you only if you buy the right one. Visit a few phone sales centers and test the various types of phones available. Also, shop around for the best plan to meet your needs.

QUICK TIP FOR HOME OFFICE PROFESSIONALS

Give your cellular phone number to only a few people. If many people are able to call you directly, you'll spend more time handling incoming calls than placing outgoing calls, and you'll see an increase in your phone bill. Clients can always reach you by pager, voice mail, or answering service.

Taking notes and maintaining phone numbers

One of the problems with using a cellular phone is that you need a place to take notes as you're talking or when you're finished with a conversation. In order to use your cellular phone to your advantage, I recommend that you do the following:

- Take notes in your daily planner during phone calls, either in the "client status" section or on the blank page facing your To-Do list. Within a PDA, use a contact manager to record notes, or create client status files. After you return to your office, transfer this information to your computer or client files.

- Use a phone log like the one in your home office to keep track of your calls.

- Use a notepad that attaches to your windshield or dashboard. Remember to remove the pages you have written on at the end of the day and to transfer the information to your To-Do list, computer, or office files. Then toss them.

- Rather than risk your life trying to drive, talk, and write notes at the same time, use a cassette recorder to make notes orally after you've finished talking on your wireless phone. Remind yourself of what was discussed and what action is needed.

- Keep all of the phone numbers you need in your daily planner, either hand-written or printed from your contact management program.

- Synchronize your desktop computer with your laptop or PDA often and you'll have a current list of client contact information with you at all times.

Pager

A pager allows your clients to reach you in minutes rather than having to wait until you check your voice mail. There are several paging options:

- The basic paging system allows others to dial a number that in turn sets off your pager and displays the number.

- A voice prompt paging system allows the caller to enter a phone number that will in turn page you. For example, your message may say, "Hi, thanks for calling XYZ company. At the tone, please enter your number and I'll return your call."

Turning Your Car Into a Functional Office

- A voice mail paging system with voice prompt allows callers to leave a voice message or phone number. If he or she leaves a message, your pager will display your pager number, which means you need to call a number to retrieve the message. Otherwise the caller's phone number is displayed so you can call them back directly.

- An alphanumeric system is a self-dispatch system you can use with your computer. The caller is greeted by an operator or answering service, who then relays the message and number to your pager.

Getting
Started

Getting Started

15

Starting anything new takes time, patience and determination. The prospect of reorganizing your work life may evoke various emotions.

Fear of failure. What if you can't get or stay organized?

Fear of success. What if you do get organized and become more productive and successful?

Anxiety. Can you accomplish everything you want to? Also, you'll have to get rid of possessions and papers you don't need but are keeping anyway.

Excitement. You're finally getting organized, or achieving a new level of organization.

This mix of emotions is a normal part of making changes in your lifestyle. It's only temporary, however. After your work life is fully organized, you'll experience joy at living with less stress, and satisfaction from having your business under control.

There are two types of people—those who do, and those who talk about doing. Those who do, plunge head first into every situation and make things happen. Those who talk about it plan far into the future but never for tomorrow. They are always waiting for the right time to make a move—when they get this or that—and never seem to make that move.

You've probably heard people say, "When I open my home office, I'll be happier," or, "When I get a new house, I'll start running my business better," or, "When I land a big client, my business will really take off." There is nothing wrong with thinking and dreaming about the future. The problem arises when you have no clear plan, just scattered ideas. Instead of saying, "When I get . . ." make a plan and follow it.

Changing bad habits

Many people can't get motivated to change their habits until they have a bad experience. For example, if you never have a checkup, you may not discover a medical problem until it is well advanced. If you consistently ignore your car's maintenance checkups, eventually your car will break down and need costly repairs that might have been avoided. After you have a bad experience like these, you might change your ways.

> Bad days are part of life, but you're a lot less likely to experience these types of setbacks if you take steps to get organized.

For a home office professional, a bad experience would be losing an account, missing an important deadline, double-booking appointments with two important clients, or appearing unprofessional in front of others.

Don't wait for something to happen to trigger you to get organized. Instead of waiting for that point, do something now to change your bad habits. Although it's easier to continue to do things the way you've always done them, there is probably a better way. Until you try it out, you'll never know what benefits being organized might bring.

In order to implement changes in your work habits, do the following:

- *Keep your personal motivation in mind.* Everyone has his or her own reason for wanting to get organized. What's yours?

- *Determine why you haven't made these changes before.* What has been holding you back? If you face this problem squarely, it may never trouble you again.

- *Recognize that you have the ability to change.* It's never too late to try something new.

- *Set goals.* The more specific your plan is, the more you will achieve.

- *Apply a new skill every day.* The more you use your new skills, the more effectively they'll work for you.

- *Reward your own good behavior.* Everybody likes positive reinforcement. When you've earned it, treat yourself.

A representative from a motivational tape company told me about a gentleman who called her and demanded his money back. He had ordered tapes from the company for years and hadn't seen any changes in his life. The woman asked him if he had done anything to make those changes, and he answered no. He thought that listening to tapes alone was going to change his life. You can be like him, and expect that simply reading this book will magically make you organized. In truth, getting organized is up to you.

Making a commitment to change

As you can tell by now, I am a firm believer in committing things to paper (or electronically). When you enter a task on your To-Do list, you are more likely to take care of it. When you list your short- and long-time goals and review these goals periodically, you will find that you accomplish more.

> When you keep track of how you use your time, you can spot time wasters you weren't even aware of before.

The first step to organizing your home office is to make an organizational plan and to commit it to paper. Use the Commitment to Change chart on page 274 to write down what changes you would like to make in your work life and why making them would be beneficial to you. Give yourself a deadline or target date to meet. Put the chart in your planner, make it a part of your computerized planning system, or post it in a prominent place in your office so that you can see what progress you are making.

COMMITMENT TO CHANGE

DATE	HABIT TO CHANGE	BENEFIT	TARGET DATE	DATE COMPLETED

©Lisa Kanarek, HomeOfficeLife.com

Staying organized

After you've organized your work life, it's unlikely you will ever return to your previous level of disorganization. The systems you set up after reading this book should suit your needs so exactly that once you get comfortable using them you will be happy to maintain them. Still, to keep motivated, it's helpful to do the following:

- Maintain a network of supportive friends and colleagues whom you trust and whose advice you value.

- Talk to others who are where you want to be. You can avoid costly and time-consuming mistakes by talking to those who have already accomplished what you want to accomplish.

- Keep updating your goals and evaluating your progress. This is best done at regular, predetermined intervals, rather than when the mood strikes you.

- Keep a positive attitude about yourself and your work.

Getting organized is possible if you combine the direction I've provided in this book with your acknowledgment that you need to make a change, your desire to change, and the action needed to implement change.

There are so many other exciting things to do in life than shuffle paper, react to hourly crises, and increase your stress level. Don't wait until it's too late. Take the time now to get organized.

Resources

The sources listed in this section provide everything from furniture to office supplies. Contact these companies by phone or via the Internet to receive more information about their products or services.

··· Furniture ···

Computer Furniture Direct
(800) 555-6126
www.cf-direct.com

Crate & Barrel
(888) 249-4158
www.crateandbarrel.com

Design Within Reach
(800) 944-2233
www.designwithinreach.com

Furnitureonline.com
1-800-407-8273
www.furnitureonline.com

Full Upright Position
1200 NW Everett
Portland, Oregon 97209
(800) 431-5134
www.fulluprightposition.com

Herman Miller for the Home
Herman Miller, Inc.,
www.hmhome.com

Ikea
(800) 434-4532 to place orders and for store locations
(410) 931-8940 East Coast
(818) 912-1199 West Coast
www.ikea.com

Knoll
1235 Water Street
East Greenville, PE 18041
(800) 445-5045
www.knoll.com

Levenger
420 S. Congress Avenue
Delray Beach, FL 33445-4696
(800) 544-0880
www.levenger.com

Lizell
P.O. Box 308
Routes 309 & 463
Montgomeryville, PA 18936
(800) 718-8808
www.lizell.com

L.L. Bean
Freeport, ME 04033-0001
(800) 544-0880
www.llbean.com

Office Depot
(888)-GO-DEPOT
www.officedepot.com

Office Furniture USA
877-FIND OFUSA (346-3638)
Officefurniture-usa.com

Office Max
(800) 788-8080
www.officemax.com

Pottery Barn
Mail Order Department
P. O. Box 7044
San Francisco, CA 94120-7044
(800) 922-5507
www.potterybarn.com

Reliable HomeOffice
P.O. Box 1502
Ottawa, IL 61350-9916
(800) 869-6000

Staples
(800) 333-3330
www.staples.com

Steelcase, Inc.
1-888-STEELCASE (for dealer network)
www.steelcase.com

Techline

500 South Division Street
Waunakee, WI 53597
(800) 356-8400
www.techlineusa.com

••• Storage & Organization •••

California Closets

(800) 873-4264
Customized, built-in systems for home offices and storage closets.
www.calclosets.com

The Container Store

(800) 733-3532
www.containerstore.com

Design Ideas (desk, file and supply organizers)

(800) 426-6394
www.desideas@eosinc.com

Design Works,Inc.

(Quick Planner -Staples sku 475368)
(413) 549-4763

Esselte Corporation

Desk accessories, filing supplies and
a wide variety of organizing products
(800) 645-6051
www.pendaflex.com

Fellowes Manufacturing Company

Makers of ergonomically correct accessories. Products
available at office supply stores.
Phone: 630.893.1600
www.fellowes.com

Get Organized
Call for catalog
(800) 803-9400
www.getorginc.com

Hold Everything
Mail Order Department
P.O. Box 7807
San Francisco, CA 94120-7807
(800) 421-2264
www.holdeverything.com

Intrigo
Makers of the Lapstation
Phone: 805-494-1742
www.intrigo.com

Iris
(800) 320-4747
www.irisusainc.com

Leeco Industries, Inc.
Portable files)
(800) 826-8806
www.cropperhopper.com

Levenger
420 S. Congress Avenue
Delray Beach, FL 33445-4696
Call or visit site for catalog
(800) 544-0880
www.levenger.com

Lillian Vernon Neat Ideas
Virginia Beach, VA 23479-0002
(800) 285-5555
Call for catalog

The Mobile Office Outfitter
1046 Sepentine Lane #306
Pleasanton, CA 94566
(800) 426-3453
www.mobilgear.com

Eldon
(800) 356-8368
www.eldonoffice.com

Organized Living
(800) 862-6556
(see listing under furniture)

Solutions
(800) 342-9988
www.solutionscatalog.com

Stacks & Stacks
www.stacksandstacks.com

••• Computer Accessories •••

APC
(surge protectors and other computer accessories)
(800) 800-4APC
www.apc.com

Computer Furniture Direct
(Oak home office furniture)
11619 Beach Blvd.
Jacksonville, FL 32246
(800) 555-6126
www.cf-direct.com

Curtis Computer Products
(800) 272-2366
www.curtiscp.com

Office Depot
(888)-GO-DEPOT
www.officedepot.com

Office Max
(800) 788-8080
www.officemax.com

Penny Wise Office Products
(800) 942-3311
www.penny-wise.com

Quill
Quill Corporation
P.O. Box 94080
Palatine, IL 60094-4080
1-800-982-3400
www.quillcorp.com

Reliable Office Supplies
P.O. Box 1502
Ottawa, IL 61350
(800) 735-4000
www.reliable.com

Staples
(800) 333-3330
www.staples.com

••• Paper-Based Planners •••

Day Runner, Inc.
> (800) 643-9923 (Day Runner Direct-to place an order)
> (800) 635-5544 (Consumer Information Center -for questions)
> *www.dayrunner.com*

Day-Timer
> (800)225-5005
> *www.daytimer.com*

Filofax
> (800) 345-6798
> *www.thedailyplanner.com*

Franklin Covey
> (800) 827-1776
> *www.franklincovey.com*

TimeDesign
> (800) 637-9942
> *www.timedesign.com*

••• Equipment & Software •••

Egghead.com
> c/o Direct Response
> P.O. Box 185
> Issaquah, WA 98027-0185
> (800) 344-4323
> *www.egghead.com*

MacConnection and PC Connection
Attn: Customer Service
450 Marlboro St.
Keene, NH 03431
1-888-213-0259
www.macconnection.com
www.pcconnection.com

MacMall
2555 West 190th Street
Torrance, CA 90504
(800) 552-8883
www.macmall.com

MicroWarehouse
1720 Oak Street
P.O. Box 3013
Lakewood, NJ 08701-5926
(800) 397-8508
www.warehouse.com

Whatever you need to know, we've made it E-Z!

Informative text and forms you can fill out on-screen.* From personal to business, legal to leisure—we've made it E-Z!

Get Out Of Debt

Made E-Z

Credit Repair

Made E-Z

Vital Records

Made E-Z

Personal & Family

For all your family's needs, we have titles that will help keep you organized and guide you through most every aspect of your personal life.

Living Wills
Includes Power of Attorney for Healthcare

Made E-Z

Asset Protection

Made E-Z

Buying/Selling Your Home

Made E-Z

Business

Whether you're starting from scratch with a home business or you just want to keep your corporate records in shape, we've got the programs for you.

Incorporation

Made E-Z

Corporate Records

Made E-Z

Accounting

Made E-Z

Your Profitable Home Business

Made E-Z

Selling on the Web (E-Commerce)

Made E-Z

Advertising Your Business

Made E-Z

* Not all titles include forms   ss 2001.r3

MADE E-Z SOFTWARE	ITEM #	QTY.	PRICE‡	EXTENSION
E-Z Construction Estimator	SS4300		$29.95	
E-Z Contractors' Forms	SS4301		$24.95	
Contractors' Business Builder Bundle	CD325		$59.95	
Asset Protection	SS4304		$24.95	
Corporate Records	SS4305		$24.95	
Vital Records	SS4306		$24.95	
Personnel Forms	HR453		$24.95	
Accounting	SS4308		$24.95	
Limited Liability Companies (LLC)	SS4309		$24.95	
Partnerships	SS4310		$24.95	
Solving IRS Problems	SS4311		$24.95	
Winning In Small Claims Court	SS4312		$24.95	
Collecting Unpaid Bills	SS4313		$24.95	
Selling On The Web (E-Commerce)	SS4314		$24.95	
Your Profitable Home Business	SS4315		$24.95	
E-Z Business Lawyer Library	SS4318		$49.95	
E-Z Estate Planner	SS4319		$49.95	
E-Z Personal Lawyer Library	SS4320		$49.95	
Payroll	SS4321		$24.95	
Personal Legal Forms and Agreements	SS4322		$24.95	
Business Legal Forms and Agreements	SS4323		$24.95	
Employee Policies and Manuals	SS4324		$24.95	
Incorporation	SS4333		$24.95	
Last Wills	SS4327		$24.95	
Business Startups	SS4332		$24.95	
Credit Repair	SW2211		$24.95	
Business Forms	SW2223		$24.95	
Buying and Selling A Business	SW2242		$24.95	
Marketing Your Small Business	SW2245		$24.95	
Get Out Of Debt	SW2246		$24.95	
Winning Business Plans	SW2247		$24.95	
Successful Resumes	SW2248		$24.95	
Solving Business Problems	SW 2249		$24.95	
Profitable Mail Order	SW2250		$24.95	
Deluxe Business Forms	SW2251		$49.95	
E-Z Small Business Library	SW2252		$49.95	
Paint & Construction Estimator	SW2253		$19.95	
MADE E-Z BOOKS				
Bankruptcy	G300		$24.95	
Incorporation	G301		$24.95	
Divorce	G302		$24.95	
Credit Repair	G303		$14.95	
Living Trusts	G305		$24.95	
Living Wills	G306		$24.95	
Last Will & Testament	G307		$24.95	
Buying/Selling Your Home	G311		$14.95	
Employment Law	G312		$14.95	
Collecting Child Support	G315		$14.95	
Limited Liability Companies	G316		$24.95	
Partnerships	G318		$24.95	
Solving IRS Problems	G319		$14.95	
Asset Protection	G320		$14.95	
Buying/Selling A Business	G321		$14.95	
Financing Your Business	G322		$14.95	
Profitable Mail Order	G323		$14.95	
Selling On The Web (E-Commerce)	G324		$14.95	
SBA Loans	G325		$14.95	
Solving Business Problems	G326		$14.95	
Advertising Your Business	G327		$14.95	
Rapid Reading	G328		$14.95	
Everyday Math	G329		$14.95	
Shoestring Investing	G330		$14.95	
Stock Market Investing	G331		$14.95	
Fund Raising	G332		$14.95	
Money For College	G334		$14.95	
Marketing Your Small Business	G335		$14.95	

‡ *Prices are for a single item, and are subject to change without notice.*

TO PLACE AN ORDER:

1. Duplicate this order form.

2. Complete your order and mail or fax to:

Made E-Z Products

384 S. Military Trail
Deerfield Beach, FL
33442

www.MadeE-Z.com

Telephone:
954-480-8933

Toll Free:
800-822-4566

Fax:
954-480-8906

continued on next page

	ITEM #	QTY.	PRICE‡	EXTENSION
Owning A No-Cash-Down Business	G336		$14.95	
Offshore Investing	G337		$14.95	
Multi-level Marketing	G338		$14.95	
Free Legal Help	G339		$14.95	
Get Out Of Debt	G340		$14.95	
Winning Business Plans	G342		$14.95	
Mutual Fund Investing	G343		$14.95	
Business Startups	G344		$14.95	
Successful Resumes	G346		$14.95	
Free Stuff For Everyone	G347		$14.95	
On-Line Business Resources	G348		$14.95	
Life Insurance	G349		$14.95	
Health Insurance	G350		$14.95	
Successful Selling	G351		$14.95	
Everyday Legal Forms & Agreements	BK407		$24.95	
Personnel Forms	BK408		$24.95	
Collecting Unpaid Bills	BK409		$24.95	
Corporate Records	BK410		$24.95	
Everyday Law	BK411		$24.95	
Vital Records	BK412		$24.95	
Business Forms	BK414		$24.95	

MADE E-Z KITS

	ITEM #	QTY.	PRICE‡	EXTENSION
Bankruptcy Kit	K300		$24.95	
Incorporation Kit	K301		$24.95	
Divorce Kit	K302		$24.95	
Credit Repair Kit	K303		$24.95	
Living Trust Kit	K305		$24.95	
Living Will Kit	K306		$24.95	
Last Will & Testament Kit	K307		$19.95	
Buying and Selling Your Home Kit	K311		$24.95	
Business Startups Kit	K320		$24.95	
Small Business/Home Business Kit	K321		$24.95	

MISC. PRODUCTS

	ITEM #	QTY.	PRICE‡	EXTENSION
☆ Federal Labor Law Poster	LP001		$5.99	
☆ State Specific Labor Law Poster (see state listings below)			$29.95	
E-Z Legal Will Pac	WP250		$9.95	

State	Item#	QTY	State	Item#	QTY	State	Item#	QTY
AL	83801		KY	83817		ND	83834	
AK	83802		LA	83818		OH	83835	
AZ	83803		ME	83819		OK	83836	
AR	83804		MD	83820		OR	83837	
CA	83805		MA	83821		PA	83838	
CO	83806		MI	83822		RI	83839	
CT	83807		MN	83823		SC	83840	
DE	83808		MS	83824		S. Dakota not available		
DC	83848		MO	83825		TN	83842	
FL	83809		MT	83826		TX	83843	
GA	83810		NE	83827		UT	83844	
HI	83811		NV	83828		VT	83845	
ID	83812		NH	83829		VA	83846	
IL	83813		NJ	83830		WA	83847	
IN	83814		NM	83831		WV	83849	
IO	83815		NY	83832		WI	83850	
KS	83816		NC	83833		WY	83851	

ORDER TOTAL ☆ Required by Federal & State Laws	$	
SHIPPING & HANDLING $4.95 for first item, $1.50 for each additional item *(All orders shipped Ground unless otherwise specified)*	$	
SUBTOTAL	$	
Florida Residents add 6% sales tax	$	
TOTAL	$	

SS 2001 r4

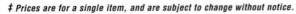

‡ *Prices are for a single item, and are subject to change without notice.*

PLEASE COMPLETE THE FOLLOWING INFORMATION:

NAME: _____

_____

COMPANY: _____

_____

ADDRESS: _____

_____

CITY: _____

STATE: _____ ZIP: _____

PHONE: ( ) _____

PAYMENT METHOD:

☐ Charge my credit card:

  ☐ MasterCard

  ☐ VISA

  ☐ American Express

ACCOUNT NO.

EXP DATE

SIGNATURE   (required for credit card purchases)

☐ Check enclosed, payable to:

Made E-Z Products
384 S. Military Trail
Deerfield Beach, FL 33442

Company Purchase Orders Are
Welcome With Approved Credit

Index

Index

Index